# PRACTICAL ELECTRONIC PROJECTS FOR MODEL RAILROADERS

## BY PETER J. THORNE

All photos, unless otherwise credited, Peter J. Thorne and Jim McCluskey

COVER AND BOOK DESIGN: Lawrence Luser
CONTINUITY: George Drury
LAYOUT: Susan Langhout

**KALMBACH BOOKS**

First printing, 1974. Second printing, 1975.

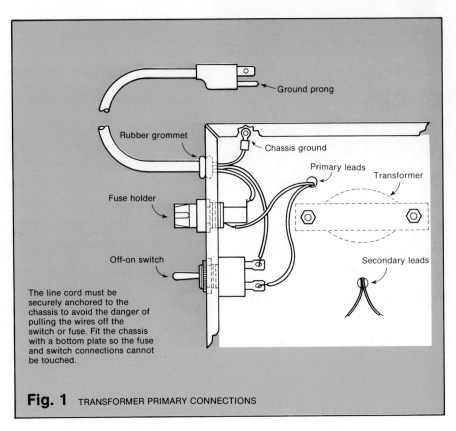

Fuse holder

Off-on switch

The line cord must be
securely anchored to the
chassis to avoid the danger of
pulling the wires off the
switch or fuse. Fit the chassis
with a bottom plate so the fuse
and switch connections cannot
be touched.

Ground prong

Rubber grommet

Chassis ground

Primary leads

Transformer

Secondary leads

**Fig. 1** TRANSFORMER PRIMARY CONNECTIONS

actually is grounded. Use your ohmmeter to measure the resistance in the circuit formed by the *ground* hole (the round one) of the wall socket and a known ground, such as a water pipe. If the resistance is low, the socket is grounded. If the resistance is high, the socket is not grounded and you should connect the metal chassis to the known ground.

Between the line cord and the primary of the transformer should be an off-on switch and a fuse. If the transformer becomes defective or the load constantly is shorted, the fuse will blow. Transformer, fuse, and switch all should be of an approved type rated for 115-volt a.c. operation. A 1-amp rating for the fuse should suffice for nearly all model railroad requirements.

The chassis must be fitted with a base plate to prevent any possibility of accidentally touching the live terminals of the switch or the fuse. If ventilation is needed for transistors or resistors under the chassis, drill some ¼" holes (smaller than a child's finger) in the base plate and the chassis. Raise the base plate from the bench by using mounting feet at the corners so air can flow upward

# ① *Safety, tools, and techniques*

IF you are a journeyman electrician or if you've been making occasional electrical repairs around the house, you will be familiar with most of the material in this chapter. Others, however, will find the information on tools useful. The techniques of laying out and making a printed circuit (PC) board are helpful to know if you plan to build several of the same type of unit.

Everyone should read the section on safety: The power pack or the transformer represents the division between scale models and the full-size world, electrically speaking, and it is a division you must always be aware of.

## Safety

Household electrical supply is nominally 115-volt a.c. This voltage can kill you if you touch a live wire while you are grounded — standing on a damp basement floor and wearing leathersoled shoes, for example.

For this reason, most of the electronic circuitry in this book is designed to operate with the safe 16-volt a.c. or d.c. output of an ordinary train power pack. A seal marked U.L. (Underwriters' Laboratories) or, in Canada, C.S.A. (Canadian Standards Association) on the power pack indicates that production samples have been rigorously checked for safety.

Some circuits need special power-supply voltages and require that you connect your own power transformer through suitable wiring to the household supply. This section describes how to do it safely. There is no reason why you cannot build your power supply to U.L. or C.S.A. standards — in fact, you owe it to yourself and your visitors to do so.

**Transformer primary circuit:** A power transformer is a necessary part of any equipment you build for operation on house current. The transformer's function is to isolate the 115-volt a.c. from the low-voltage secondary circuit, which you can handle safely. The primary of the transformer is connected to the household supply at the wall socket with a flexible insulated line cord, an off-on switch, and a safety fuse. These components must be an approved type, and they must be wired carefully.

Additionally, when the equipment is in a metal box or on a metal chassis, this metal must be connected to a ground. Thus, if your wiring is faulty and the house current is connected to your metalwork, the fuse in the household circuit will blow, protecting you and the equipment.

Grounding is best done through the third conductor of the line cord and a grounded wall socket. You may want to make sure that the ground of the socket

through the chassis. Never remove the base plate without completely disconnecting the equipment from the house current. If you are using a power transformer with exposed terminals, put the entire transformer in a ventilated metal enclosure, unless you can mount it so that the terminals all project into the underside of the chassis.

**Anchoring the line cord:** Always mechanically secure the line cord to the chassis. A sharp tug on the cord could pull off an unsecured soldered connection. You can use small plugs and sockets, as on a radio, so that a pull results in a disconnection. Put the male part of the set on the chassis, as on small household appliances, so live prongs won't be exposed.

The line cord must be in no danger of chafing against a metal surface. Therefore it must pass through a plastic or rubber grommet as it enters the chassis. Several kinds of plastic combination grommet-and-clamp devices are available.

Don't knot the line cord on the inside of the chassis to prevent it from being pulled through. The insulation may eventually crack because of the tight radius of the knot.

**Fuses and overload trips:** Fig. 2 shows samples of fuses, fuse holders, and circuit breakers. The circuit breaker is a

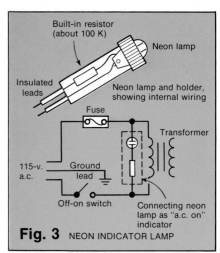

**Fig. 3** NEON INDICATOR LAMP

Kalmbach Books: A. L. Schmidt

Fig. 2. Left to right: fuse in fuse holder, fuse alone, and circuit breaker. The HO scale box car provides an excellent indication of the size of the components.

thermo-mechanical device that opens the circuit when an excessive current flow overheats a bimetal strip. The circuit stays open until the breaker is reset by pushing in the reset button. A blown fuse must, of course, be replaced.

Circuit breakers can be used in the 115-volt primary circuits as well as in the low-voltage secondary, but they are more useful in the latter because of accidental short circuits on the track caused by derailments and the like.

**Neon safety tester:** A miniature neon lamp lights up at 50 volts or so and draws a very low current. It can be used as a safety checker to ensure that equipment connected to the a.c. line is safe before permanent installation on the layout. The neon lamp also can be used as an indicator light to show that the a.c. line is connected (fig. 3). Both types must have built-in series resistors.

To use the lamp as a safety checker, connect one lead to a ground first and then carefully place the other lead on the output terminals of the equipment. If

the lamp lights, current is leaking from the primary side of the transformer to the low-voltage side of the device. Similarly test the chassis and the cover.

## Tools

If you have done any wiring at all, you probably already have needle-nose pliers, diagonal wire cutters, and a soldering iron. In addition to these items, it's useful to have a mechanical wire stripper, cooling clips to use as heat sinks during soldering, and a general purpose multimeter.

**Wire stripper:** Most of the projects in this book require quantities of wire leads. A mechanical insulation stripper (fig. 4) can save you time and do a better job than a knife. The stripper cuts the insulation and removes it from the wire in one simple squeeze operation (fig. 5). A knife can cut off strands in stranded wire; knife nicks in solid wire can cause the wire to break when it is bent. The mechanical wire stripper eliminates both these problems.

**Soldering tools:** For soldering small components, a miniature-type soldering iron with a high-heat element in the 40- to 50-watt range is best (fig. 4). The hot tip ensures a rapid solder joint. Even if you already have a soldering iron, you may want to look at a newer one. In the past several years solid-state devices have replaced transformers in soldering tools, making them lighter and easier to use.

Fig. 6 shows the difference in appearance between good and bad solder joints. Always use 60/40 (60 per cent tin, 40 per cent lead) resin-cored solder. Never use an acid or paste flux; these eventually corrode the wires.

**Soldering techniques:** Use care in making solder connections to semiconductors. Either too much heat or the proper heat too long can permanently damage the device. Always observe these precautions when you solder a semiconductor:

● Solder as far as convenient from the body of the semiconductor.

● Never apply molten solder or a hot soldering tool to a lead or a terminal for more than 10 seconds or nearer than ⅛" to the body of the device.

● Keep the surfaces to be soldered clean and the tip of the iron tinned so

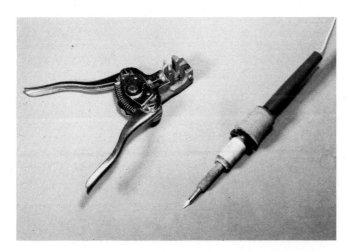

Fig. 4. A wire stripper and a pencil-type soldering iron will be among your most frequently used tools.

Kalmbach Books: A. L. Schmidt

Fig. 5. A wire stripper removes insulation neatly and quickly, and it prevents nicks and cut-off strands.

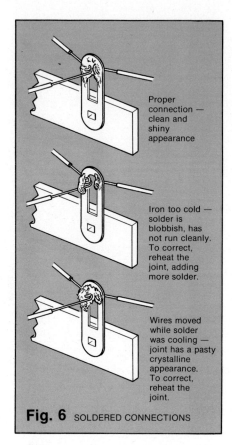

Proper connection — clean and shiny appearance

Iron too cold — solder is blobbish, has not run cleanly. To correct, reheat the joint, adding more solder.

Wires moved while solder was cooling — joint has a pasty crystalline appearance. To correct, reheat the joint.

**Fig. 6** SOLDERED CONNECTIONS

the connection can be made as quickly as possible.

● Grip the lead to be soldered with a cooling clip. This keeps the semiconductor crystal cool during the soldering process. Fig. 7 illustrates a cooling clip in use. The particular one illustrated is made by X-acto. It hangs on by spring pressure, leaving your hands free.

**Meters:** A small multi-range meter is useful for testing resistors and insulation continuity and generally checking the wiring of a layout. The lower-priced imported meters can be purchased for as little as $10; fig. 8 shows a better-quality multi-range meter. The ranges shown on the dial are typical; however, the lower-priced meters cannot read very low currents. This is not a drawback in model railroading, nor do we need a high-sensitivity meter — 1000 ohms per volt is more than adequate.

Possibly you can acquire a low-priced, basic, 1-ma. or 5-ma. d.c. meter, which

Fig. 7. A cooling clip, shown clamped onto the lead of a diode, absorbs excess heat from the soldering iron.

you can adapt to read 16 volts full scale by connecting it in series with a resistance of 16,000 or 3100 ohms, respectively.

By adding an adjusting potentiometer in series with a fixed resistance and a 1.5-volt battery, you can also use the meter movements to measure resistance (fig. 9). Adjust the potentiometer so the meter reads full scale with the test leads joined. If the test leads are connected across a resistor the meter reads less than full scale. You can calibrate the scale using known values of external resistance. Note that the scale is not linear but is cramped at the left end.

### Printed circuit boards

There are two common ways to construct the electronic devices described in this book. One way is to fasten tag strips to a piece of hardboard and solder the components to the lugs of the tag strips. The wire leads of the components are stiff enough so the components remain in position.

The other way is to use a printed circuit (PC) board, a piece of plastic with copper foil bonded to it in a pattern that forms part of the wiring between the components. The use of PC board results in a neater-looking device, and it makes mass-production of such items as signal modules much easier.

Because PC boards are specified for a number of projects in this book, the technique of making PC boards is important enough to discuss here.

The usual method of making a PC board involves creating a negative opaque to ultraviolet light, either by drawing the layout several times the required size and reducing it photographically or by cutting an adhesive ruby-colored film to size. The copper foil on the board is treated with a photo-resist material and then exposed to ultraviolet light through the negative. Then the photo resist is developed, to protect the copper in the etching process, and the unwanted copper is etched away.

Fig. 8. A high-quality multimeter such as this one is a handy tool if you intend to do much electronics work.

There are other methods. You can carefully grind away unwanted copper with a motor tool or use adhesive-backed copper strips and blank boards. Kits for making PC boards can be purchased with all the materials you need. Check the catalog of the electronics supply houses such as Allied and Lafayette.

**Circuit layout:** Some wiring diagrams in this book have layouts for a PC board. To make a negative, lay the ruby film over a full-size layout of the board. Then cut the film along the outline of the circuit connecting lines. A swivel knife works nicely for this. Remove the circuit paths (remember, you are making a negative) by gently lifting one edge of the film with a pair of tweezers and pulling it away from the sheet. Mark the holes to be drilled in the completed board with a dot of India ink. If you make a mistake, either make a new negative or use a special tape to patch the area and recut it.

**Board preparation:** Cut the board to size before the printing process to prevent damage to the board or the conductors. Clean the foil thoroughly with household cleanser and a rag or sponge, and wash away all traces of the cleanser with hot water. Pat it dry with a clean

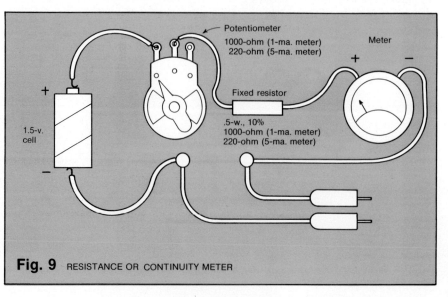

+

Potentiometer
1000-ohm (1-ma. meter)
220-ohm (5-ma. meter)

Meter

1.5-v. cell

−

Fixed resistor

.5-w., 10%
1000-ohm (1-ma. meter)
220-ohm (5-ma. meter)

+ −

**Fig. 9** RESISTANCE OR CONTINUITY METER

Fig. 10. A swivel knife facilitates the task of cutting the curved circuit paths in the ruby film.

Fig. 11. Lift the cut area of the ruby film with tweezers. The clear area represents the copper on the finished board. The ink dots become uncoppered areas on the board and are the location of the mounting holes for the components.

Fig. 12. Position the artificial negative over the sensitized copper-clad board, and then use an ultraviolet lamp to project the image of the negative onto the board.

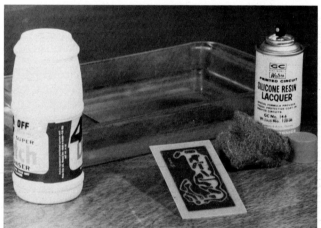

Fig. 13. Use a glass baking dish to hold the etchant. After the board has been etched, use steel wool and scouring powder to polish it. Silicone resin lacquer keeps the surface clean.

paper towel and let it air-dry, or spin it dry on an old phonograph turntable with built-up edges. Do not touch the clean foil with your fingers, as this causes smudging and spotting.

**Photo-resist application:** While a darkroom is not necessary, handle the photo-resist material in a dim light. Some precautions are necessary: good ventilation, no smoking, and no open flame. Wear rubber gloves to protect your hands during the etching process. Be sure to read the directions that come with the various chemicals.

Apply the photo-resist to the foil by pouring it over the board or by dipping the board into a glass tray filled with resist. Drain off the excess and air-dry or spin-dry the board in a dust-free place. Air-drying takes about an hour; spin-drying, about half an hour. If you are not going to use the board immediately, store it in a dark, moisture-proof vinyl bag. Be careful not to scratch the resist coating.

**Exposure:** Place the negative face down in a printing frame, and place the foil side of the laminate in position on the negative. Exposure time is not critical with film negatives, because the thin film prevents creepage and undercutting of the lines by the ultraviolet light. A fixture holding two 15-watt ultraviolet lamps at approximately 10″ from the frame does the job in about 5 minutes.

**Developing:** Immediately after exposure, transfer the board to a glass tray filled with photo-resist developer, foil side face up. Agitate the solution constantly by gently raising and lowering one end of the tray for 2 to 3 minutes. Remove the board and rinse it under a

Fig. 14. You can use self-adhesive conductive strips and blank phenolic board to make a circuit board.

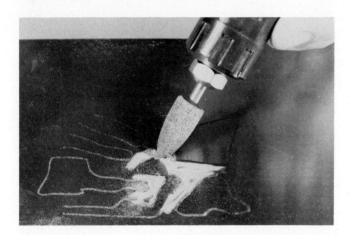

Fig. 15. Another quick way to make a circuit board is to trace the outline of the circuit on the board and grind away the unwanted copper. Be careful not to grind through the board. Wear safety glasses for all grinding operations.

hot water tap. At this point you can see the pattern faintly on the foil. You can save the developing solution in an airtight container and reuse it several times.

**Etching:** Two types of etchants in particular lend themselves to a small operation: ammonium persulfate and ferric chloride. Both are readily available and neither produces toxic fumes. Mix the etchant in the proper proportions and pour it into a glass tray or jar. Place the board in the solution face up and agitate the tray or jar until all the unwanted copper foil is etched away, which can take anywhere from 5 to 20 minutes, depending on solution strength, temperature, and the amount of agitation. Rinse the completely etched board in hot water.

**Finishing:** Clean the foil with photoresist thinner to remove any remaining resist. Polish it with household cleanser or fine steel wool to ensure good soldering. The board now is ready for drilling and wiring. In order to properly position component holes and prevent damage to the backing, drill from the foil side with a small drill as a pilot. Use only light pressure to prevent damage to the backing. Continue drilling with the proper size drill when the pilot holes are done. A No. 55 drill suffices for wire clearance for most of the components specified in this book.

To speed the drilling process in a small production run, make a template with holes flared to guide the drill. Fix the template in place on several boards and clamp the stack together tightly. Then you can drill several boards in one operation.

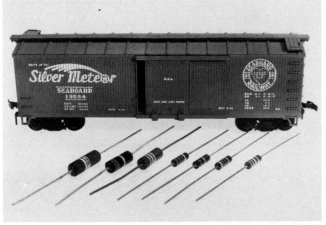

Kalmbach Books: A. L. Schmidt

Fig. 1. Three 1-watt fixed resistors, left, and four .5-watt fixed resistors, right. For size comparison, the box car is HO scale.

Kalmbach Books: A. L. Schmidt

Fig. 2. Left: two potentiometers, each with an sp.st. switch mounted on the rear; right: a 50-ohm rheostat.

# ② *Components*

YOU can ignore this chapter if you already are familiar with resistors, capacitors, transistors, and the like. However, you may find the information useful if your local electronics store wants to offer you a substitute for the items specified in the parts list; you may be able to debate with the store on its own terms.

This is not to suggest that substitutions are not in order; indeed, there are so many different manufacturers of components that specifying a list of parts for a project that can be obtained from just one source is almost impossible.

On the other hand, if electronics is new territory for you, this chapter can give you some idea of what the various components do and what they look like.

## Resistors

A resistor is a device which resists the flow of electric current. In model railroad electronics it can be regarded as a voltage-reducing component. Certain parts of a transistor circuit may need, say, 12 volts for operation; another section of the same circuit may need 4 volts; and a third, 6 volts. Resistors are used to drop from the maximum of 12 to the 4-volt and 6-volt levels required.

**Resistor construction:** Resistors of 2-watt rating or smaller are usually carbon rod material enclosed in an insulating jacket. Occasionally a minute carbon film is applied in a spiral pattern on a ceramic tube and the assembly is coated with insulating lacquer.

Above 2 watts the wire-wound resistor is more common. Resistive wire is wound on a tube and then sealed in a ceramic rod. The surface of this type of resistor can become quite hot to the touch. In some cases the wire-wound resistor is not sealed in ceramic material and the wire, usually Nichrome, can be seen.

Overheating and damage show up as discoloration of the paint or as a split casing with sealed resistors.

**Fixed resistors:** Fig. 1 shows a variety of fixed resistors. The value of a fixed resistor is nearly always given by colored bands around one end of the resistor. See the table. (There is a slightly off-color sentence to help you remember the table: almost anyone in electronics can tell it to you.)

The unit of resistance is the ohm, which sometimes is abbreviated with the Greek letter omega. The letter K (for kilo) indicates 1000 ohms. The higher the value, the more the voltage is dropped, other factors being equal. A resistor has a value of 1 ohm if it produces a voltage drop of 1 volt when a current of 1 amp flows through it. This equation is Ohm's Law, $R = E/I$, where R is the resistance in ohms, E is the voltage, and I is the current in amperes.

**Variable resistors:** If a resistance element is made in a doughnut shape, a wiper can be added to make the resistance variable. The voltage at the wiper depends on its position.

Variable resistors are known as either rheostats or potentiometers. Rheostats generally are larger and have two terminals, one on the slider and the other at one end of the resistance. Potentiometers have three terminals, one on the slider and one at each end of the resistance.

Wire-wound potentiometers are more expensive and have a higher wattage rating than the carbon-track types. Wire-wounds are used in the better-quality power packs; carbon-tracks in transistor throttles. Both types are used for speed control. Miniature preset carbon types adjustable with a screwdriver are available for applications in which adjustment seldom is needed.

Often seen is a dual-control or twin-gang potentiometer, with two separate tracks controlled by a single knob. This type of control can be used as a combined speed and pulse-amplitude control for a transistor throttle.

**Wattage:** All resistors dissipate heat. An electric heater is a resistance designed specifically for that purpose: A 1000-watt heater is nothing more than a large 14.4-ohm resistor. A more common size resistor for our purposes is 15-ohm, .25-watt, which is about 4000 times smaller.

The largest resistor used in model railroading is the wire-wound speed control of the conventional throttle. This control is a variable resistor that must carry the locomotive current, about 1 amp in HO scale and more in the larger sizes. It can dissipate as much as 20 watts and consequently can become hotter than a 15-watt lamp.

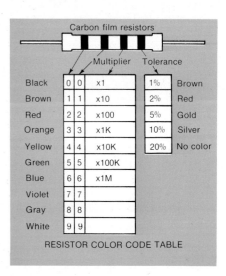

| Carbon film resistors | | | | |
|---|---|---|---|---|
| | | Multiplier | Tolerance | |
| Black | 0 0 | x1 | 1% | Brown |
| Brown | 1 1 | x10 | 2% | Red |
| Red | 2 2 | x100 | 5% | Gold |
| Orange | 3 3 | x1K | 10% | Silver |
| Yellow | 4 4 | x10K | 20% | No color |
| Green | 5 5 | x100K | | |
| Blue | 6 6 | x1M | | |
| Violet | 7 7 | | | |
| Gray | 8 8 | | | |
| White | 9 9 | | | |

RESISTOR COLOR CODE TABLE

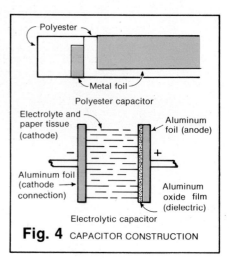

Fig. 4 CAPACITOR CONSTRUCTION

Fig. 3. Left to right: two electrolytic capacitors, a ceramic disk capacitor, and a paper capacitor.

Fixed resistors are available with various wattage ratings; .25, .5, 1, 2, 5, and 10 are common values. In general, the physical size of the resistor varies with the wattage, although the material used can make a difference. There is no harm in using a higher rating than specified if the physical size of the resistor is not a problem, but never use a rating lower than specified.

**Calculation of wattage:** The wattage rating necessary for a resistor can be calculated in any of three ways: EI, $I^2R$, or $E^2/R$, where E, I, and R are the voltage across the resistor, the current through it, and the resistance of the resistor.

To take a practical example, suppose you need to supply two grain-of-wheat building lights from a 20-volt transformer. Each lamp draws about .05 amp at 12 volts. Placing the lamps in parallel makes the total current draw .1 amp. The resistor must drop 8 volts. Its resistance — R = E/I — is 80 ohms. Its wattage — EI — is .8, so a 1-watt or 2-watt resistor is necessary.

Strictly speaking, you can't apply Ohm's Law to a.c. circuits, but it works reasonably well for low frequencies.

**Testing resistors:** Nearly all general purpose multimeters have a scale that can be used to measure resistors directly. Don't try to measure a resistor that is in a circuit, since other components may be wired across it, and you could possibly damage a transistor in this way. Disconnect one end of the resistor before you check it with the meter.

## Capacitors

The basic unit of capacitance is the farad (fd.), although the values we are concerned with are so small that the microfarad, one millionth of a farad, is the common unit. It is abbreviated mfd. A lower-case Greek mu is also correct instead of the m for micro. Extremely small values are expressed in picofarads (pfd.), one millionth of a microfarad.

Electrolytic capacitors range in value from 10,000 mfd. down to about .5 mfd. Paper and polyester types range from 5 mfd. to .005 mfd., and ceramic disk capacitors from .05 mfd. down to .0001 mfd.

In its simplest form a capacitor consists of two conductive plates facing but not touching each other. A pair of cymbals an inch or so apart form a 200-pfd. capacitor with a 30,000-volt rating (assuming they are held by something other than your hands). Nonconductive material other than air between the two plates increases the capacity; this material is called a dielectric. Paper, polyester, ceramic, and mica capacitors have a layer of that material between layers of conductive foil. Electrolytic capacitors rely on a very thin layer of aluminum oxide formed by the interaction of electric current and an electrolyte inside the capacitor. Since capacity varies inversely with the distance between the two plates, the electrolytic type has a higher capacity for a given size, with the penalty, though, that the electrolytic type must be connected to the circuit with the correct polarity. The other types can be connected either way.

**Uses of capacitors:** Capacitors, often still referred to as condensers, have two properties that are related to each other: They can store and release electrical energy, and they can pass alternating current while blocking direct current. They have a number of uses in model railroading: They serve as filters for rectifiers, they store energy for operating switch machines, and they are an essential part of the momentum circuit in the transistor throttle described in Chapter 4.

Capacitors are available with voltage ratings ranging from 3 to 600 or so. For model railroad applications, 25-volt or 50-volt electrolytic and 50-volt or 100-volt polyester types are suitable. Most small ceramic and mica types carry a 250-volt rating. The voltage rating is the maximum direct voltage that can be safely applied across the capacitor. The higher the voltage rating for a given value capacitor, the larger and more expensive it will be. There is no harm in using a higher voltage rating than is specified, and with an electrolytic type this leads to a longer life for the capacitor.

Electrolytic capacitors tend to lose capacity over a period of years as the chemical solution inside dries up. Also, after a long period of disuse an electrolytic capacitor may have a reduced capacity but will restore itself after a few minutes of use. Reduced capacity is evidenced by absence of momentum on a transistor throttle or a reduced maximum speed. You can check this by connecting a good capacitor across the suspected unit; there's no need to disconnect the old one from the circuit.

Electrolytic capacitors are used in power supplies to yield pure d.c. from the pulsating output of rectifiers. This application generates internal heat in the capacitor, depending on the amount of current drawn from the power supply. If the capacitor is specified with a ripple current rating, choose a type with the rating about twice the d.c. output of the power pack. When no ripple current rating is available, use a physically large capacitor. Don't mount electrolytics too close to heat sources, such as power transformers. Avoid using tantalum capacitors, which tend to overheat in power-supply circuits because of their small size.

**Tolerance:** For other than electrolytics, capacitors come in 10 per cent and 20 per cent tolerances. The 20 per cent rating is satisfactory for all the circuits in this book. When in doubt use the next larger capacitance value.

Nearly all electrolytics have a tolerance, usually unstated, of —10 to + 50 per cent. Again, if a quoted value of capacitance is not available, use the next larger.

**Bipolar electrolytics:** As noted above, electrolytics are polarized and must be connected with correct polarity. For some applications, such as locomotive sound circuits, electrolytics must be used to block the train running power in both directions since the required capacitance precludes the use of other types. Connect two electrolytics cathode-to-cathode as shown in fig. 5. The capacitors should be of the same type; the effective capacity is half that of one unit. You also can purchase bipolar electrolytics, which are simply two electrolytics, back-to-back.

**Testing capacitors:** You can check a capacitor for short circuits with the resistance scale of a simple multimeter. In general, a capacitor should show a high resistance to d.c. The electrolytic type tends to show a low resistance that increases rapidly to a high value. Observe the polarity when you test electrolytic types. The internal battery of the meter is nearly always connected to the test leads with reverse polarity.

### Diodes

A diode is one of the simplest items of electronic hardware. In basic terms it is a piece of semiconductor material with two wires or leads called the anode and the cathode. A diode passes electricity in one direction only. If the positive terminal of a battery is connected to the anode, the diode allows current to pass, but if the positive terminal of the battery is connected to the cathode, no current passes.

If alternating current is applied to a diode, then direct current comes out. In a power pack, diodes are used to convert the 16-volt a.c. output of the transformer to d.c. for the permanent-magnet motors in the locomotives. In this application a diode, or a group of them, is called a rectifier.

**Diode materials:** Three materials are used for diodes. Selenium is not as common now as it was. Germanium still is common for small diodes; the price is low and several circuits in this book specify germanium diodes for other than rectifier applications. Most power-supply rectifier diodes are silicon. The cooling fins on the selenium bridge rectifiers are not needed for silicon rectifiers, because the silicon crystal in the diode can operate safely at a higher temperature than a selenium or germanium crystal. The case of a silicon diode will be warm, but it should never become too hot to touch.

Small-signal (low-voltage, low-current) diodes usually are encased in epoxy plastic or clear or painted glass. The larger diodes (1-amp and above) for rectifier use have metal cases with glass seals for the leads. Up to 1 amp the epoxy plastic type is suitable for model railroading purposes because the case is

large enough for good cooling and is insulated to avoid accidental short circuits with other wiring.

**Rectifier circuits:** The simplest rectifier circuit is a single diode, as in the first line of fig. 6. It permits half the a.c. to pass and blocks the other half moving in the opposite direction. This rectifier circuit is called a half-wave rectifier. It is not used much, except in some power packs with a pulse-full switch. In pulse position, part of the more efficient type of rectifier in the power pack is bypassed and the circuit becomes a half-wave rectifier.

If you use two diodes to supply the d.c. line from both sides of the a.c., as in the second line of fig. 6, you have a full-wave rectifier. The full-wave rectifier is more efficient because it leaves no large gaps in the output wave form. The transformer used for the full-wave rectifier is a center-tapped-secondary type. If you trace the circuit, you will see that only half the secondary winding of the transformer is working at any one time.

The most widely used type of rectifier is the bridge rectifier. With four diodes and a single transformer winding without taps, performance is the same as the full-wave rectifier. Moreover, the diodes

in the bridge rectifier need only half the current rating of those in the full-wave rectifier. Fig. 7 shows a typical bridge rectifier. The diodes are mounted down between the square plates that serve as cooling fins. Silicon bridge rectifiers may consist of four diodes or may be a single unit.

**Connecting diodes:** Bridge rectifiers nearly always are marked with a sine-wave symbol at the a.c. end, where the leads may be connected to the trans-

Fig. 7. A typical selenium bridge rectifier. The square fins are for cooling.

Connect two electrolytic capacitors of the same capacity and working voltage.

**Fig. 5** BIPOLAR CAPACITOR

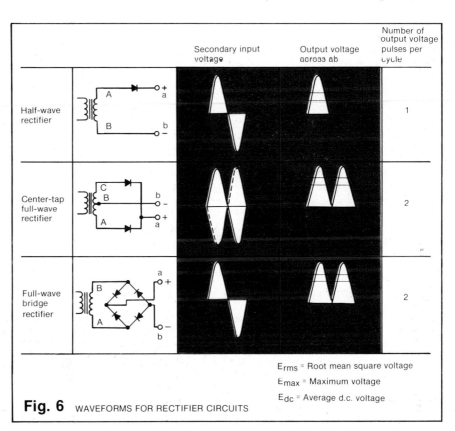

| | | Secondary input voltage | Output voltage across ab | Number of output voltage pulses per cycle |
|---|---|---|---|---|
| Half-wave rectifier | | | | 1 |
| Center-tap full-wave rectifier | | | | 2 |
| Full-wave bridge rectifier | | | | 2 |

$E_{rms}$ = Root mean square voltage
$E_{max}$ = Maximum voltage
$E_{dc}$ = Average d.c. voltage

**Fig. 6** WAVEFORMS FOR RECTIFIER CIRCUITS

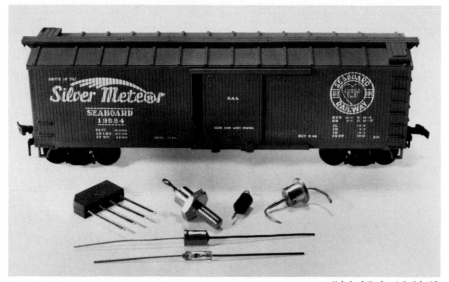

Kalmbach Books: A.L. Schmidt

Fig. 8. A silicon bridge rectifier (the rectangular-cased item with four leads) and five silicon diodes of various sizes and configurations.

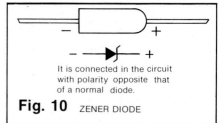

It is connected in the circuit with polarity opposite that of a normal diode.

**Fig. 10** ZENER DIODE

former either way, and with a plus and a minus at the d.c. end. Sometimes the plus and minus are replaced with dots of red and black paint, respectively.

Single diodes sometimes are coded with symbols to indicate polarity. The metal-cased miniature top-hat diodes almost invariably have the hat brim as the cathode connection. (Current flows through if you connect the anode to the positive side of the power supply and the cathode to the negative.) The screw-thread-mounted type usually has the cathode connected to the screw. The plastic-cased type with one end tapered has the cathode at the pointed end, so current flows in the direction of the point. Other types may have a band of color at the cathode end. Consult the data for that type if you're in doubt, or test them gently with your multimeter.

**Output voltage:** One of the more confusing aspects of power-supply rectifiers is reconciling the d.c. output voltage with the a.c. input voltage. A detailed explanation is beyond the scope of

this book. Consider, though, that the transformer is putting out a.c. with a voltage that varies from zero to the maximum output voltage, both forward and back, many times a second; the rectifier is converting this to pulse d.c., which also varies from zero to maximum at the same frequency; the diodes waste some energy as heat; and the output voltage of the transformer drops as current is drawn from it. Obviously less energy will emerge from the d.c. terminals than enters at the a.c. end.

To get 12-volt pulsating d.c. from a half-wave rectifier, the transformer must be rated at 26 volts. For a full-wave rectifier, you need a 27-volt center-tapped transformer (also known as 13.5-0-13.5-volt). With the bridge rectifier, 14-volt a.c. produces 12-volt d.c.

Selenium diodes lose a little more voltage than silicon diodes do. The traditional power pack feeds 16-volt a.c. to a selenium bridge rectifier to get 12-volt d.c. for running the trains; the same 16-volt a.c. is tapped, naturally, for auxiliaries such as lights and switch machines.

**Ratings:** Diodes are specified by a voltage rating and a current rating. Other ratings for diodes are of no interest to model railroaders unless you plot your trains with radar.

The voltage rating is termed the piv rating (peak inverse voltage). In rectifier applications the piv rating required is 1.4 times the a.c. input voltage plus the d.c. output voltage plus 10 per cent for high line-voltage conditions. Thus even a 16-volt a.c. rectifier circuit requires diodes with a piv rating of (16 x 1.4 + 22.5) x 1.1, or about 50.

Selenium rectifiers rated below 50 piv cost less than those rated above 50 piv. Silicon diodes have a similar change in price structure at about 200 piv. Consider, though, the safety factor in using a diode with the highest economical peak inverse voltage rating.

The low-current germanium and silicon diodes used in the circuits in this book generally need only a 25-piv rating, because they are used only in d.c. circuits. The parts lists specify the ratings needed.

In rectifier circuits with a capacitor input filter, the maximum usable current rating for the diodes often is only 75 per cent of the published ratings. Check the manufacturer's data if you are in doubt.

Diode heat is a concern only when the diodes are used for O gauge power packs. Selenium diodes carry their own cooling fins. Silicon diodes develop less heat; at 1 amp the silicon diode develops about .5 watt. No special cooling is needed other than to avoid obstruction of cooling airflow. As mentioned earlier, 1-amp diodes are sufficient for a 2-amp power pack, but for O gauge, 2-amp diodes are needed to carry the heavier motor current. These usually are stud-mounted types on a small metal plate for cooling. Carefully insulate either the mounting stud from the metal or the metal cooling plate from the other components.

The small-signal germanium and silicon types used in the magnetic relay track detector circuit and the full performance throttle discussed later develop little or no heat because of the small currents involved, and no precautions for temperature are needed.

If a selenium bridge rectifier fails, you will detect the vile cat odor that results. Silicon and germanium diodes give no outward sign of failure, except perhaps for melting or cracking of the plastic case.

Radio interference on rare occasions can be caused by a silicon rectifier diode. If this happens you can cure it by connecting a 1000-pfd. (.001-mfd.) ceramic capacitor across the diode. The capacitor does not affect the operation of the rectifier but bypasses transient high-frequency pulses.

Zener diodes pass current freely in one direction but restrict the flow to a certain voltage in the other. They are used in two circuits in this book to provide a stable voltage where the current in the circuit can vary. The symbol is slightly different from the symbol for the conventional diode (fig. 10) and zener diodes always are connected backwards compared to ordinary diodes; that is, the positive supply goes to the cathode of the zener diode. Normally the zener diode is used on d.c. only. It is identified

**Fig. 9** RECTIFIER CIRCUITS

by its reference voltage and the heat it can dissipate. The zener diodes used in the circuits in this book are small ones, 2 watts or less. Heat sinks are not necessary at the low-power ratings.

## Transistors

A transistor is a two-junction three-layer semiconductor device that can amplify current, voltage, and power. For the purposes of this book you need not know exactly what happens inside a transistor, but a brief discussion of how it works may help you to understand how the circuits in this book work and what to expect when things go wrong.

All transistor circuits essentially are simple in principle, like the one in fig. 13. They often look complicated because additional devices are connected into the circuit.

A transistor has three terminals: collector, base, and emitter. Two circuits are involved. They use a common path through the emitter, but they are separate through the base and the collector. The transistor, basically, senses any change in the base circuit and regulates the collector circuit accordingly, but over a much wider range. A multiplication factor between 50 and 100 is common. You can view the transistor as an electrical lever, or consider the base circuit a pygmy master and the collector circuit a giant slave.

In fig. 13, the regulating element is a rheostat, but it could be a switch, a potentiometer, a photocell, or any other device that can develop or modify a current. The load in the circuit can be a lamp, a motor, or any other device that uses current.

The circuit of fig. 13 shows the transistor regulating current through the load. It is more useful, though, to regulate voltage across the load. To do that requires only that the load be placed between the emitter and the power source.

**Transistor ratings:** In model railroading we are concerned with power dissipation, voltage and current ratings, gain, and leakage current of transistors. We usually don't have to worry about noise and frequency specifications.

Never use a transistor with a voltage rating lower than 25 for collector-emitter voltage with open base. Medium-gain transistors (with a gain rating of 20 or more for power transistors; 50 or more for smaller devices) are suitable, except for O gauge throttles, which call for high-gain devices.

Recommended minimum values for collector current (d.c., not peak) are .1 amp for small transistors, .5 amp for medium transistors, 3.5 amps for germanium power transistors, and 10 amps for silicon power transistors.

The dissipation rating indicates the maximum continuous heat the device can dissipate safely. Different manufacturers specify it differently, and it may be only a theoretical value that presup-

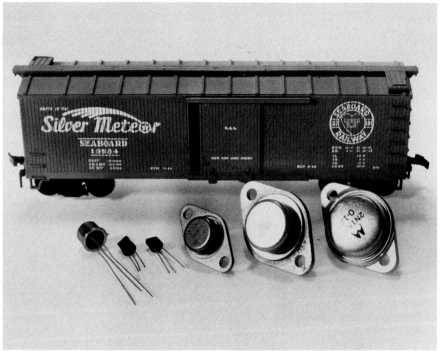

Kalmbach Books: A.L. Schmidt

Fig. 11. An assortment of transistors. In general, the larger the case of a transistor, the higher the power rating of that transistor. NPN and PNP transistors look alike.

## RECOMMENDED TRANSISTOR TYPES

The transistors listed here are only a small cross-section of suitable devices and manufacturers. All the types listed have an excellent safety margin for the uses in this book. JEDEC types are usually available from several sources; the other numbers are house types and are listed in alphabetical order.

| Low-power Silicon NPN | | Case Type | Medium-power Silicon PNP | | Case Type |
|---|---|---|---|---|---|
| JEDEC | 2N697 | TO-5 | JEDEC | 2N2905 | TO-5 |
| | 2N2222 | TO-18 | | 2N3502 | TO-5 |
| | 2N3302 | TO-18 | Elcom (Canada) | ES68 | TO-126 |
| Amperex | A157 | TO-18 | Matsushita/National | 2SA546 | TO-39 |
| Elcom (Canada) | ES20 | TO-18 | Motorola | HEP242 | TO-5 |
| Matsushita/National | 2SC538 | TO-18 | Philips (Canada) | BD135 | TO-126 |
| Philips (Canada) | BC107 | TO-18 | R.C.A. | SK3025 | TO-5 |
| R.C.A. | SK3020 | TO-1 | Sylvania | ECG129 | TO-5 |
| Sylvania | ECG123A | TO-18 | **High-power Silicon NPN** | | |
| **Low-power Silicon PNP** | | | JEDEC | 2N3055 | TO-3 |
| JEDEC | 2N2907 | TO-18 | Elcom (Canada) | ES31 | TO-3 |
| | 2N2696 | TO-18 | Matsushita/National | 2SC647 | TO-3 |
| Amperex | A177 | TO-18 | Motorola | HEP247 | TO-3 |
| Matsushita/National | 2SA550 | TO-18 | Philips (Canada) | BDY20 | TO-3 |
| Philips (Canada) | BC177 | TO-18 | R.C.A. | SK3027 | TO-3 |
| **Low-power Germanium PNP** | | | | 40633 | TO-3 (plastic) |
| JEDEC | 2N1372 | TO-5 | | | |
| | 2N2428 | TO-1 | Sylvania | ECG130 | TO-3 |
| | 2N2431 | TO-1 | Texas Instruments | TIP33 | TO-3 (plastic) |
| Elcom (Canada) | ES4 | TO-1 | **High-power Germanium PNP** | | |
| Matsushita/National | 2SB346 | TO-1 | JEDEC | 2N1553 | TO-3 |
| Motorola | HEP633 | TO-1 | | 2N2869 | TO-3 |
| Philips (Canada) | AC128 | TO-1 | | 2N301 | TO-3 |
| R.C.A. | SK3004 | TO-1 | | 2N441 | TO-36 |
| Sylvania | ECG102A | TO-1 | Elcom (Canada) | ES21 | TO-3 |
| **Medium-power Silicon NPN** | | | | ES10 | TO-36 |
| JEDEC | 2N2270 | TO-5 | Matsushita/National | 2SB129 | TO-3 |
| | 2N2297 | TO-5 | Philips (Canada) | AD149 | TO-3 |
| | 2N3053 | TO-5 | | ADZ11 | TO-36 |
| | 2N3109 | TO-5 | R.C.A. | SK3009 | TO-3 |
| Elcom (Canada) | ES22 | TO-5 | | SK3012 | TO-36 |
| Matsushita/National | 2SC696 | TO-39 | Sylvania | ECG121 | TO-3 |
| Motorola | HEP243 | TO-5 | | ECG105 | TO-36 |
| Philips (Canada) | BD136 | TO-126 | **High-power Silicon PNP** | | |
| R.C.A. | SK3024 | TO-5 | Texas Instruments | TIP34 | TO-3 |
| Sylvania | ECG128 | TO-5 | | | |

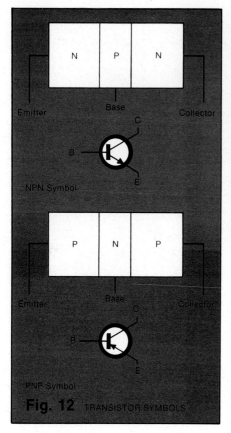

**Fig. 12** TRANSISTOR SYMBOLS

N P N

Emitter — Base — Collector

C
B
E

NPN Symbol

P N P

Emitter — Base — Collector

C
B
E

PNP Symbol

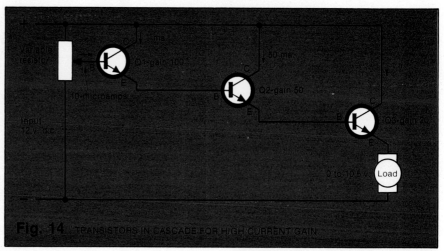

**Fig. 14** TRANSISTORS IN CASCADE FOR HIGH CURRENT GAIN

Variable resistor

1 ma.

50 ma.

Q1-gain-100

Q2-gain-50

Q3-gain 20

10-microamps

Input 12 v. d.c.

0 to 10.5 v

Load

poses infinitely efficient cooling. If possible, find a rating for the device at ambient temperature or mounting-plate temperature of 45°C. The ratings sometimes published for cooler temperatures are much higher and may be misleading. Recommended minimum ratings are .2 watt for small transistors, .8 watt for medium-power transistors, and 40 watts for high-power transistors.

The parts lists for the projects in this book specify suitable transistors. In addition, a table gives a selection of transistors available at reasonable prices. Note that the list is only a small sample of those available; there are many other manufacturers with equivalent devices.

**Transistor leakage:** All transistors show a small amount of leakage in the

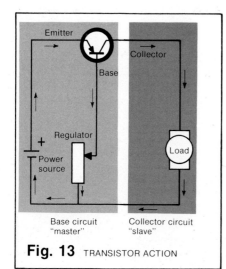

Emitter

Collector

Base

Regulator

Load

Power source

Base circuit "master"

Collector circuit "slave"

**Fig. 13** TRANSISTOR ACTION

input circuit. This leakage depends on temperature and acts to reduce the bias on the transistor and increase its collector current. The device becomes hotter, producing more leakage, and the process, called thermal runaway, continues until the transistor self-destructs.

Careful circuit design can eliminate leakage effects entirely: Good signs are low resistances between base and emitter, and resistance in series with the emitter. Leakage is more likely to be a problem with germanium devices or off-brand transistors than with silicon; beware of bargain-price assortments. In circuits carrying very low current, little or no leakage protection is needed.

**Connections:** Transistors come in a wide variety of cases and connections, but most of the ones used in this book are of the types shown in fig. 15.

All power transistors have the collector connection bonded internally to the metal case or to the mounting lug. The case can be conveniently used to cool the transistor. Fig. 16 shows the mounting hardware needed. Note the mica insulating washer and the silicone grease which provide electrical insulation while permitting cooling. Fig. 17 shows various kinds of cooling clips and heat sinks.

If you should substitute a transistor that is not an exact replacement, make sure the connections are the same as the specified device.

**Testing transistors:** For proper testing you need complex equipment, but fig. 18 shows how to get a reasonable indication of whether the device is good or bad by using an ohmmeter. Often the easiest way to check a component is to replace it with a known good one and see if the circuit works better.

## Transformers

A transformer consists of two coils of wire wound around a laminated iron core. Its function is to reduce 115-volt house current to a safe voltage for model railroad purposes. The primary coil or winding, which is connected to the

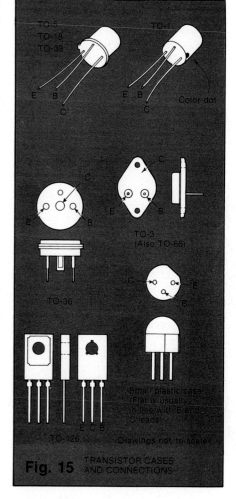

TO-5
TO-18
TO-39

TO-1

E B C

E B C

Color dot

C

E B

C

E B

TO-3 (Also TO-66)

TO-36

C

B

E

E C B

TO-126

Small plastic case (Flat is usually in line with E and C leads)

Drawings not to scale

**Fig. 15** TRANSISTOR CASES AND CONNECTIONS

house current, has about 2500 turns of thin enamel-insulated copper wire; the secondary winding has fewer turns — the number is in proportion to the output voltage — of thicker wire. Some transformers have taps at various points on the secondary coil; others may have more than one secondary. In common-rail layout wiring, it is necessary for each throttle to have either a separate transformer or a separate secondary.

Transformers are rated by secondary voltage and current. Fig. 19 shows three transformers, each with a 12.6-volt secondary. The smallest, with a .5-amp rat-

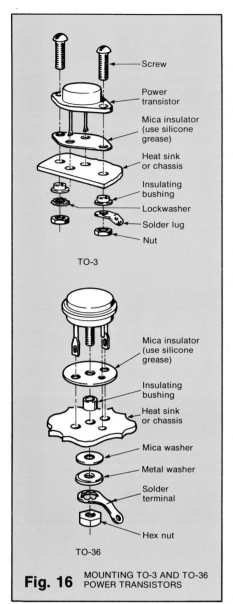

**Fig. 16**  MOUNTING TO-3 AND TO-36 POWER TRANSISTORS

*(labels in figure, top TO-3):*
Screw
Power transistor
Mica insulator (use silicone grease)
Heat sink or chassis
Insulating bushing
Lockwasher
Solder lug
Nut
TO-3

*(labels in figure, bottom TO-36):*
Mica insulator (use silicone grease)
Insulating bushing
Heat sink or chassis
Mica washer
Metal washer
Solder terminal
Hex nut
TO-36

Fig. 17. Clip-on heat sinks such as these absorb and dissipate heat from transistors.

### WIRE SIZES AND CHARACTERISTICS

| Wire size AWG | Copper | | | Nichrome |
| --- | --- | --- | --- | --- |
| | Diameter (inches) | Ohms per 100 feet 68°F | Safe current in amperes in closed space* | Ohms per foot |
| 12 | 0.080 | 0.16 | 15 | 0.092 |
| 14 | 0.064 | 0.25 | 13 | 0.146 |
| 16 | 0.051 | 0.40 | 10 | 0.233 |
| 18 | 0.040 | 0.64 | 8 | 0.370 |
| 20 | 0.032 | 1.02 | 5 | 0.589 |
| 22 | 0.025 | 1.61 | 4 | 0.936 |
| 24 | 0.020 | 2.57 | 3 | 1.49 |
| 26 | 0.016 | 4.08 | 2 | 2.37 |
| 28 | 0.013 | 6.49 | 1.5 | 3.76 |
| 30 | 0.010 | 10.3 | 1.3 | 5.98 |
| 32 | 0.008 | 16.4 | *In free air | 9.52 |
| 34 | 0.006 | 26.1 | safe current | 15.1 |
| 36 | 0.005 | 41.5 | is twice that | 24.1 |
| 38 | 0.004 | 66.0 | for closed space. | 38.3 |
| 40 | 0.003 | 104.9 | | 60.8 |

AWG wire sizes  22  20  18  16  14  12

ing, is suitable for use with a transistor throttle for N scale operation. The middle one is rated at 1 amp, suitable for small HO locomotives, and the largest, rated at 4 amps, can handle O gauge engines. The physical size of a transformer is a function more of its current-carrying capacity than of its secondary voltage.

**Voltage drop:** A transformer secondary winding has some resistance, since it consists of many yards of copper wire, and the transformer also has a small resistance that depends on the ratio of the primary voltage to the secondary voltage. This all means that the more current drawn, the lower the output voltage. For example, a small transformer might produce 16 volts at no load and 12 volts at .5 amp. A larger transformer usually has a proportionally lower voltage drop. Partly as a consequence of this, transformers run warm; some types can run up to 80°C core temperature.

The voltage drop of a transformer sometimes is used indirectly as a safety factor, as in a transistor throttle. When a transistor throttle is short-circuited, a heavy current flows through the power transistor, which would overheat if the voltage remained at its level. However, as current through the transformer increases, the voltage drops because of transformer resistance, and the heat overload is shared between the transformer and the transistor. The moral here is to never use a transformer with a greater current rating than necessary.

Because transformers generate heat, keep them away from transistors and diodes.

### Switches

Two types of switches are used in model railroading: toggle and rocker switches, with spring-loaded action, and

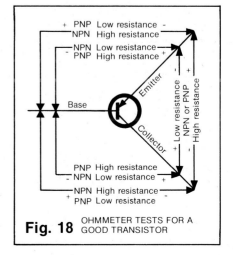

*(labels in figure):*
+ PNP Low resistance –
NPN High resistance
– NPN Low resistance
+ PNP High resistance +
Base
Emitter
Collector
– Low resistance NPN or PNP +
+ High resistance –
PNP High resistance
– NPN Low resistance +
– NPN High resistance
+ PNP Low resistance –

**Fig. 18**  OHMMETER TESTS FOR A GOOD TRANSISTOR

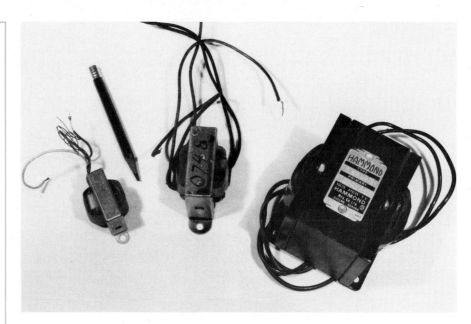

Fig. 19. Left to right: transformers for 12-volt output at .5 amp, 1 amp, and 4 amps.

Kalmbach Books: A. L. Schmidt

Fig. 20. Clockwise from top: a rotary switch (viewed from the back), a toggle switch, a slide switch, and two rocker switches. The last four look alike from the rear.

rotary or wafer switches (fig. 20). Toggles were classics for many years, but they gradually are being replaced by plastic rocker-action switches. They have the same function, and they look almost the same from the back.

Toggle and rocker switches are available in a.c.-only versions, with a slow make-and-break switch action, and a.c.-d.c. versions, with a quick switch action. The latter is preferable for model railroad uses. Switches are rated by voltage and current, such as 6 amps at 125 volts. A switch with that rating is suitable for any normal model railroad use.

Use rotary or wafer switches in low-current, low-voltage circuits only, since the contacts are smaller and easily could be damaged by high currents and voltages. If you use a rotary switch for progressive cab control, for example, be sure the switch can carry the motor currents.

**Switches for house current:** Always use an enclosed-type toggle or rocker switch for switching house current. Never use a rotary or wafer switch, as the high voltage would soon cause the contacts to arc over and melt.

**Switch shorthand:** Each separate switchable circuit is called a pole. The number of positions on the switch to which each pole can be connected is termed the number of throws or ways. The common reversing switch is a two-pole, two-throw switch, abbreviated to 2p.2t. or dp.dt. (for double pole, double throw). Rotary switches have anywhere from 2 to 11 ways, and the number of poles can be increased by adding switch sections up to the length of the central rotating bar.

### Wire

No. 22 AWG (American Wire Gauge) solid wire is the best for wiring electronic components. This wire is commonly available with a PVC (polyvinyl chloride) insulation in a variety of colors.

Stranded wire is good in tight quarters, as for rotary switches, since it puts less strain on the thin switch connections than solid wire does. Be careful that you don't accidentally cut off several strands of the wire when you strip off the insulation.

For long connections, use larger diameter wire to avoid a voltage drop because of the resistance of the wire.

When you connect switch machines, try to have no more than .25 ohm in the connecting leads. Thus No. 14 AWG wire, at .25 ohm per 100 feet, can carry current for a switch machine 50 feet from the power source. (Remember that the current must go out and come back.) With a capacitor discharge unit, even less resistance is desirable. If you don't have heavy wire available, try doubling up the wiring with two lengths of smaller diameter wire.

# ③ Circuits with diodes

MANY model locomotives have a headlight, and some also have a rear-mounted backup light. Prototype practice usually is to light only the lamp facing the direction of travel. This can be done automatically on models by using a diode in series with each lamp.

The convention for track polarity is that the positive supply is on the right-hand rail facing in the direction of travel. For the headlight to light in the forward direction, a diode is connected in series with one of the lamp leads, with its anode connected to the motor lead that picks up current from the right-hand rail. The other lamp lead is connected to the motor lead supplied from the left-hand rail. The backup light is connected the same way, but with the di-

ode reversed. Fig. 1 gives a diagram, and fig. 2 shows a photograph of the diodes installed in a model.

Diode ratings are not particularly important in this application. The diodes in the photograph are 100-volt, 1-amp silicon diodes in epoxy cases. Smaller glass-encapsulated diodes are suitable for N scale locomotives. The minimum acceptable rating for this application is 50 volts and 1 amp, but that size is not likely to be any cheaper.

Mount the diodes on the frame of the locomotive in any convenient place, using epoxy cement to hold them. You can cut off the diode leads about ½" from the body of the diode and solder flexible insulated wire to the stub, using a cooling clip to keep from overheating the di-

ode. Avoid using a metal-cased diode, because the metal case is the cathode connection and could cause a short circuit if it touched the metal frame of the locomotive.

**Problems?** If the lamps light in the wrong direction, just exchange the lamp leads at the diodes.

The diodes work on both filtered and pulsed d.c., but both lamps will light simultaneously if you are using a constant-lighting generator (Chapter 8).

## Constant lighting for locos

All diodes have a small voltage drop across their terminals when current is passed through them. This drop does not change with current as happens with a simple resistance, where the voltage drop is proportional to the current. A silicon diode has a voltage drop of .7 volt over its usable current range; two in series give a drop of 1.4 volts. You can take advantage of this property to get constant headlight brightness. Place two pairs of diodes in series with the motor, one pair pointing in each direction, and wire a 3-volt lamp across the set of diodes (figs. 3 and 5).

This is what happens: When 2 volts is applied to the rails, the diodes drop 1.4 volts, leaving only .6 volt for the motor. This is not enough voltage to run the

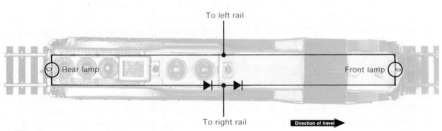

**Fig. 1** AUTOMATIC HEADLIGHT SWITCHING

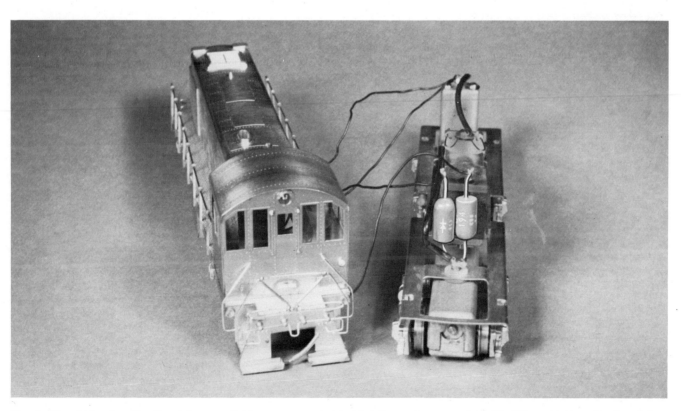

Fig. 2. The diodes for directional lamp switching are mounted behind the motor magnet of this HO scale Alco diesel switcher.

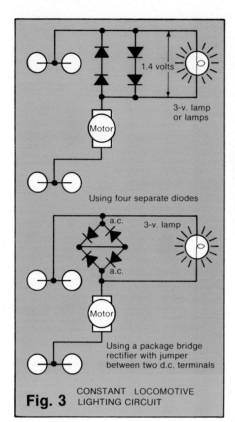

Using four separate diodes

1.4 volts

3-v. lamp or lamps

Using a package bridge rectifier with jumper between two d.c. terminals

**Fig. 3** CONSTANT LOCOMOTIVE LIGHTING CIRCUIT

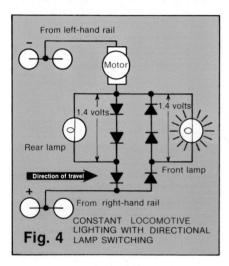

From left-hand rail

1.4 volts    1.4 volts

Rear lamp

Direction of travel

Front lamp

From right-hand rail

**Fig. 4** CONSTANT LOCOMOTIVE LIGHTING WITH DIRECTIONAL LAMP SWITCHING

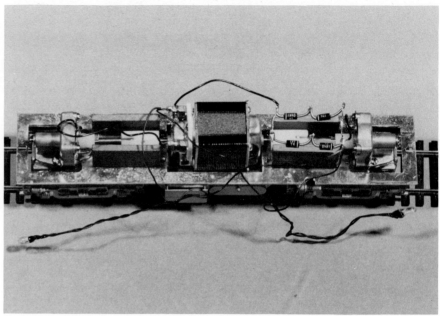

Fig. 5. The diodes for the circuit of fig. 3 are epoxied to the frame of this HO diesel.

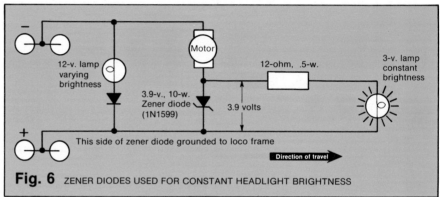

12-v. lamp varying brightness

3.9-v., 10-w. Zener diode (1N1599)

3.9 volts

12-ohm, .5-w.

3-v. lamp constant brightness

This side of zener diode grounded to loco frame

Direction of travel

**Fig. 6** ZENER DIODES USED FOR CONSTANT HEADLIGHT BRIGHTNESS

motor, but the lamp gets 1.4 volts and burns with a fair brilliance. All you have to do is crack the throttle a bit to turn on the light without running the locomotive. When you increase the throttle to 5 volts, the diodes still drop 1.4 volts, leaving 3.6 volts to start and run the motor. The headlight gets 1.4 volts. At full throttle the motor gets 10.6 volts, which is usually enough for full-scale speed; the lamp still receives only 1.4 volts.

The system works equally well on pulsed or filtered d.c. However, locomotive running power must be connected to the track for the lamp to light.

**Directional constant lighting.** Fig. 4 shows how the constant lighting circuit can be modified for directional switching by adding two more diodes. This circuit works well, but it is virtually impossible to install in N scale engines.

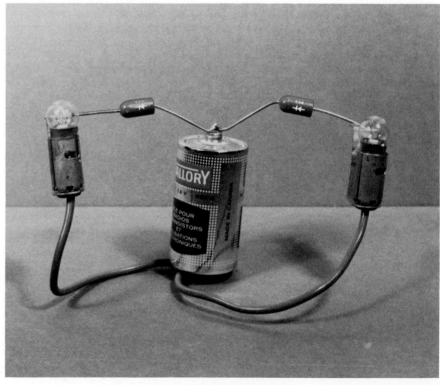

Fig. 7. One battery, two diodes, and two lamps illustrate how diodes conduct current.

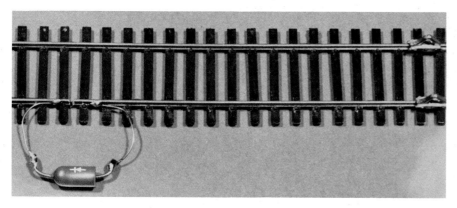

Fig. 8. The diode connected across the gap stops any locomotive heading toward the end of the track once its wheels are to the right of the gap; power can still reach the locomotive to back it out of the dead-end spur.

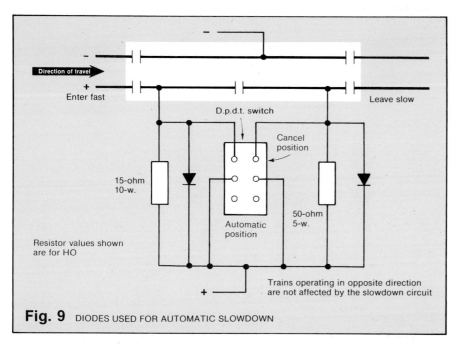

Fig. 9 DIODES USED FOR AUTOMATIC SLOWDOWN

Labels within figure:
- Direction of travel
- + Enter fast
- Leave slow
- D.p.d.t. switch
- Cancel position
- 15-ohm 10-w.
- 50-ohm 5-w.
- Automatic position
- Resistor values shown are for HO
- + Trains operating in opposite direction are not affected by the slowdown circuit

**Zener diode constant lighting:** A simpler wiring installation is possible using a zener diode, such as International Rectifier No. 1N1599 (fig. 6). The zener diode gives a constant drop of 3.9 volts when connected in reverse polarity. In the opposite direction only a low voltage drop occurs, so that with a 3-volt lamp and a 12-ohm resistor (or a 6-volt lamp) connected across the zener diode, enough voltage to light the lamp is obtained. The rear lamp can be switched on and off with a conventional diode, or a second zener diode can be added for constant lighting in both directions.

The 1N1599 is rated at 10 watts and generates 4 watts of heat when used with a 1-amp motor. The device must be cooled by mounting it on the locomotive's metal frame, which normally is connected to the right-hand rail.

Because of the physical size of the zener diode, this circuit is not suitable for N scale. Remember also that the voltage at the motor is 3.9 volts less than the voltage at the power pack terminal, so with some low-geared models you may want to make a 3-volt to 4-volt increase in the maximum throttle setting.

**Diode ratings:** Diodes used in series with lamps need a .1-amp, 100-piv rating. Motor diodes, though, carry the full motor current and should be rated for .5 amp, 1 amp, and 3 amps for N, HO, and O scales, respectively.

## Diodes for track control

You can use the diode's property of unidirectional conduction to stop a locomotive before it reaches the end of a track. Cut a gap in one rail about one locomotive-length from the end of the track and wire a diode across the gap so that current can reach to the end of the track only if it is of the polarity for backing a locomotive out (fig. 8). Use a 1-amp silicon diode for N and HO; use two in parallel for heavy O scale motors. You can, of course, conceal the diode below the layout board, connecting it to the track with feeder wires. Don't solder it together until you have tested and made sure the diode is pointed properly.

**Automatic slowdown:** You also can use diodes for an automatic slowing circuit, such as you might use through the diverging route of a facing-point turnout. Fig. 9 shows the circuit. The north side of the track is negative for a train heading east. Under these conditions, the diodes connected in series with the sub-blocks on the south side of the track do not conduct, so the current for the train must go first via a 15-ohm resistor and then through a 50-ohm resistor. These give a substantial speed reduction. When the train travels in the opposite direction, the diodes conduct and the full operating voltage reaches the train. The toggle switch lets you cancel the automatic slowdown. You can omit the switch, but there is a possibility of a slow-running locomotive stalling with the 50-ohm resistor in the circuit. To start a stalled train, just flip the cancel switch or open the throttle.

The diodes carry the full motor current and should be rated accordingly. Both of these circuits remain effective with lighting or sound power connected to the track, provided all rail gaps are bridged with a capacitor.

**Automatic stopping and starting:** A stop-and-start circuit is useful for setting up automatic operation on part of the layout or perhaps on a trolley line that circles the village. One of the simpler methods of stopping and restarting a train is to use a negative-temperature-coefficient resistor, as shown in fig. 10.

The NTC resistor has a high resistance when cold and a low resistance when hot. Thus a locomotive entering a block fed through such a device stops because of the resistance in series with the motor. As current flows through the NTC resistor and the stalled motor, the device heats up, its resistance drops, and more current flows, eventually starting the motor. When the train moves out of the block the resistor cools down for the next cycle.

The Philips/Amperex NTC resistor No. E215AB/P150E has a resistance of 150 ohms cold and perhaps a tenth of that hot. For a typical HO motor, restart takes 20 to 30 seconds, and cooling time is about 30 seconds. Cooling can be speeded up by mounting the NTC resistor on a piece of aluminum. A 20- to 50-ohm, 5-watt potentiometer can provide fine adjustment.

The reason for using 16-volt a.c. and a diode to supply the stopping block is to guarantee restart. A low throttle setting might not provide enough voltage through even the hot NTC resistor to restart the locomotive. Moreover, the pulsed d.c. results in better starting.

## Dimming lights

The circuit of fig. 11 shows how a diode can be used to dim yard and building lights to about half normal brightness. The switch gives full brightness in one direction; in the other direction, the diode allows only alternate half cycles of a.c. to pass. A 1-amp diode is sufficient to light 20 or so grain-of-wheat lamps.

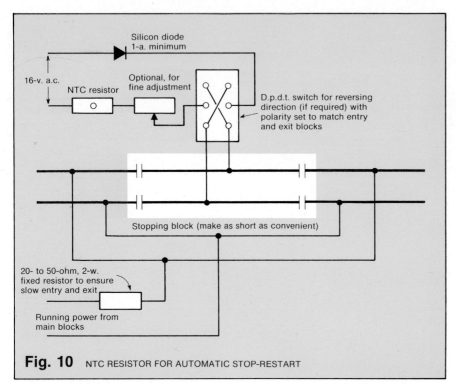

**Fig. 10** NTC RESISTOR FOR AUTOMATIC STOP-RESTART

Silicon diode
1-a. minimum

16-v. a.c.

NTC resistor

Optional, for fine adjustment

D.p.d.t. switch for reversing direction (if required) with polarity set to match entry and exit blocks

Stopping block (make as short as convenient)

20- to 50-ohm, 2-w. fixed resistor to ensure slow entry and exit

Running power from main blocks

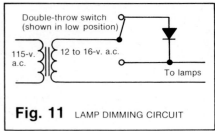

Double-throw switch (shown in low position)

115-v. a.c.

12 to 16-v. a.c.

To lamps

**Fig. 11** LAMP DIMMING CIRCUIT

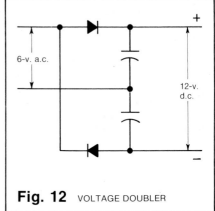

6-v. a.c.

12-v. d.c.

+

−

**Fig. 12** VOLTAGE DOUBLER

The circuit can be used only with a.c.

The advantage of the diode over a resistor is twofold. First, the diode dissipates little or no heat, as compared to the 5-watt resistor needed for the same effect in a 1-amp circuit. Second, the brightness difference between full and half remains constant with the diode "wattless dropper," whether one lamp is connected or several are. With a resistor, the more lamps added, the dimmer each becomes.

### Filtered d.c.

Nearly all power supplies for electronic model railroad equipment must provide filtered or pure d.c. This is because transistors often perform switching functions, and the transistors would confuse ripple or variations in the supply voltage with the signal that controls the transistor.

The ripple is removed by a high-value electrolytic capacitor across the d.c. output terminals. The capacitor acts as a reservoir, storing up energy during output troughs. The output usually is referred to as filtered d.c.

The addition of the capacitor increases the d.c. voltage. Whereas a single diode gives about 45 per cent d.c. voltage from a given a.c. input, and full-wave and bridge rectifiers give about 90 per cent, the addition of a large filtering capacitor gives up to 140 per cent d.c. from a given a.c. input voltage.

This apparent magnification is put to use in Chapter 5 to make increased energy levels available for a snap-acting switch-machine power supply. However, something for nothing is not the case here. Even though the voltage increases, the power must remain constant. Therefore the continuously available current

is a bit lower when a filter capacitor is added to the rectifier output.

Another diode circuit of interest is the voltage doubler. One version is shown in fig. 12. This circuit gives, for example, 12 volts filtered d.c. output at 1 amp from a 6-volt, 2-amp input transformer. The two capacitors should be identical. (For the example shown, 500 mfd. at 15 wvdc is a suitable rating.)

A basic filtered d.c. power supply is shown in fig. 13. The values of the components change according to the output requirements; the table lists them along with suitable transformers.

Most of the designs in this book have been calculated for supply from the nominal 16-volt a.c. terminals of an ordinary power pack. The power pack is the most readily available safe and economical source of low-voltage a.c.

For relay control circuits, the d.c. voltage depends on the type of relay

used. The track detection circuits of Chapter 6 can be used over a wide range of d.c. input voltage so that the magnetic relay coils can be selected for price and availability. The d.c. voltage used for the transistor circuitry can be that required by the relay.

None of the transistor-only circuits in this book requires more than 1 amp, with the exception of a signal installation with more than 20 signals. The track detection circuits with relays draw current in proportion to the number of relays and their resistance.

### Diodes for circuit protection

Transistor circuits can be damaged if the power supply is connected with incorrect polarity. A diode can be connected in series with one lead of the unit, so that if the power supply is reversed the diode will not conduct and no damage can result.

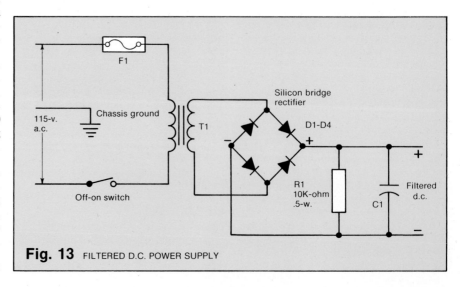

F1

115-v. a.c.

Chassis ground

T1

Off-on switch

Silicon bridge rectifier

D1-D4

−

+

R1 10K-ohm .5-w.

C1

Filtered d.c.

+

−

**Fig. 13** FILTERED D.C. POWER SUPPLY

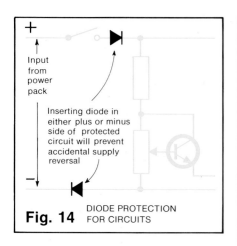

**Fig. 14** DIODE PROTECTION FOR CIRCUITS

Inserting diode in either plus or minus side of protected circuit will prevent accidental supply reversal

Input from power pack

You may connect the diode in the positive lead, with the anode toward the power supply positive, or in the negative lead, with the cathode toward the power supply negative (fig. 14). An example of this is found in Chapter 4, in the simple transistor throttle circuit. The diode carries the full-load current of the protected circuit and must be rated accordingly.

**Transistor throttle indicator:** Two diodes and two lamps can be used as a combined voltage output indicator and reverse polarity indicator on transistor throttles. One diode (D1 in fig. 3) conducts when the throttle is working normally, and the 16-volt lamp in series lights up in proportion to the output voltage and the train speed.

Accidental connection of another throttle to the same block can damage a transistor throttle, if the two voltages are in opposite polarity. If this happens, diode D2 conducts, causing warning lamp L2 to light up. When that happens, you should disconnect power from the track until the fault is cleared. The diodes and lamps must be connected on the throttle side of the reversing switch as shown.

## COMPONENTS FOR FILTERED D.C. POWER SUPPLY

| Output | T1 | F1 rating | C1 rating | D1-D4 rating* |
|---|---|---|---|---|
| 15 to 18 volts at 1 amp | 12.6- to 13-volt secondary: Chicago-Stancor TP-1 Hammond (Canada) 166J12 | .25-amp | 1000-mfd., 15-wvdc | 1-amp, 200-piv |
| 21 to 25 volts at 1 amp | 18- to 20-volt secondary: Chicago-Stancor TP-1 Hammond (Canada) 166J20 | .5-amp | 1000-mfd., 25-wvdc | 1-amp, 200-piv |
| 33 to 35 volts at 1 amp | 25-volt secondary: Chicago-Stancor P6469 Hammond (Canada) 166J25 | .5-amp | 1000-mfd., 35-wvdc | 1-amp, 200-piv |
| 12 to 14 volts at 3 amps | 10-volt secondary: Chicago-Stancor P8380 Hammond (Canada) 167N10 | 1-amp | 4000-mfd., 15-wvdc | 2-amp, 200-piv |

*The diode rating is for each silicon diode. You may substitute a bridge rectifier package, such as Varo VE27 or the Philips BY164 for 1-amp circuits and Varo VH247 or G.I. KBS02 for 3-amp circuits.

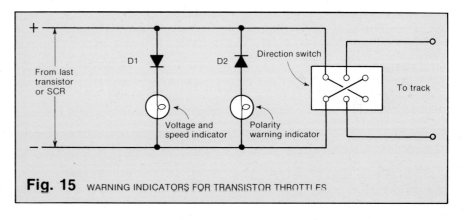

**Fig. 15** WARNING INDICATORS FOR TRANSISTOR THROTTLES

# ④ *Throttles you can build*

ALTHOUGH most of us start with a packaged train set, we quickly progress to more sophisticated equipment. The train-set couplers are replaced with smooth-acting knuckle types, carefully lubricated with graphite. The roundhouse soon shelters a couple of nicely weighted brass imports with balanced 5-pole motors. Our new equipment is capable of slow-motion coupling moves, smooth starts, and prototypical acceleration.

Now is the time for a power supply that is more advanced than a simple power pack. Now is the time to achieve prototypical operation with a transistor throttle (or a solid-state or SCR throttle). You can't get as good a slow-running action, all things being equal, with any other type of throttle. You can't simulate 200 tons of inertia as well any other way. You can't get such a simple and effective braking action with any other throttle.

## Questions and answers

**Why use transistors?** In a conventional power pack (fig. 1) motor speed is controlled by connecting a variable resistance, a rheostat, in series with the motor. The higher the resistance, the lower the voltage at the motor and the slower the motor runs.

The problem with rheostat control involves the starting characteristics of the motor. The motor draws more current just before it starts to turn than it does after it has started. Take an example: A particular engine starts at 3 volts. Before the wheels turn it draws .6 amp, and after it starts it draws .5 amp. The rheo-

stat dissipates about 9 volts before the engine moves and at the same setting dissipates only 7.5 volts when the engine is in motion. There is a voltage increase from 3 volts to 4.5 volts just as the engine begins to move, and as a result it immediately accelerates to 15 scale mph or so. To eliminate this effect the voltage must be independent of the current.

To improve this situation, make the throttle resistance zero by opening the rheostat all the way. Then feed the full-throttle voltage into a transistor, as in fig. 2. The transistor has three leads: base, collector, and emitter. Two of them, the collector and the emitter, are connected into the main current path. The voltage applied to the base causes the transistor to allow almost the same voltage through the collector-emitter circuit whether the motor is turning or not. The result is the same as with a variable transformer to control voltage but at lower cost and a smaller physical size.

Fig. 3 shows the details of a control circuit that applies the voltage to the base of transistor Q1. This circuit uses an additional small transistor to gain leverage. The result is that a low-cost potentiometer, R1, can control the voltage easily without danger of burning out. The two safety diodes, D1 and D2, need some explanation. D1 ensures that only pulses of correct polarity are permitted to enter the transistor throttle; reverse current might damage the transistors. If you get no output from the transistor throttle, reverse the direction switch on the power pack. Train direction now is controlled by the reversing switch on the transistor throttle. D2 helps prevent

damage on twin-cab layouts where another throttle of reverse polarity can accidentally be connected across the transistor throttle. When this happens, D2 bears the load, dropping the voltage of the other throttle. Don't leave things in this state too long, or D2 will become hot. D2 also keeps reverse polarity transients from damaging transistor Q1. This can occur when a high-inductance motor is intermittently connected to the track, as can happen with dirty rails.

**Are transistor throttles reliable?** Some early transistor throttles may have been underdesigned so that, for example, control was lost when the throttle was warm because of prolonged running. A good design from any well-known manufacturer should have a large reserve capacity for overload. All the circuits in this book have protection built in.

**What are the important ratings of a transistor throttle?** The most important rating is the current rating, usually expressed in amps. The size you need depends on your scale and whether you double-head locomotives. For double-heading in N scale, a 1-amp rating is sufficient. In HO scale a double-headed train draws up to 2 amps, as does a two-motored locomotive. For the larger scales check the actual rating of the motor. A.H.M.'s O scale equipment produced after 1970 by Rivarossi draws no more current than an HO locomotive does, but other O scale locomotives may draw as much as 3 amps per motor. Double-heading requires a 6-amp throttle, which is expensive to build and nearly impossible to buy because of the cost of transistors capable of passing high currents. The highest-rated throttle in this book is a 3-amp model.

**What is an SCR throttle?** It's one in which the main-power transistor is replaced by a silicon controlled rectifier (SCR). The extra components needed make it more complicated than the transistor throttle. This book describes an SCR throttle for HO gauge.

The SCR, also known as a thyristor, needs much less cooling than a transistor because it operates only in pulses. This apparent advantage has a drawback: The

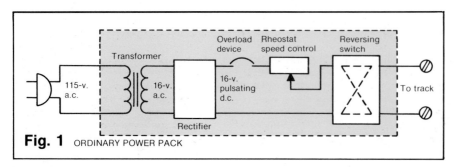

**Fig. 1** ORDINARY POWER PACK

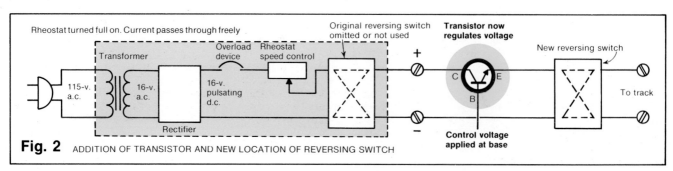

**Fig. 2** ADDITION OF TRANSISTOR AND NEW LOCATION OF REVERSING SWITCH

motors used in our models overheat with full-speed pulse-only operation. Drive wheels tend to skitter on the rails and become polished, and the motor commutator may in time blacken and become pitted.

There is a cure. A large-value paper or electrolytic capacitor added across the output of an SCR throttle filters and reduces the spiky pulses. The effect of the capacitor is, however, not completely controllable, since the amount of pulse reduction depends on the current being drawn from the throttle.

**Can an ordinary throttle be converted into a transistor throttle?** No, but the transistor part of the throttle can be added externally to the ordinary throttle. The ordinary throttle is used only to supply the input voltage to the transistor section; all control operations then are done in the add-on transistor part.

An example of this technique is shown in this book. The advantage of the add-on throttle is that all the high-voltage wiring has been done by the manufacturer of the power pack to an approved safety standard. Only low voltage remains for you to work with.

**Are transistor throttles complicated to handle?** You will find that when a throttle has several control knobs only two or three are used frequently. These are the speed control, the brake, and the reversing switch.

Some people like to make minor adjustments frequently; others do not. You can select the throttle you make or buy on the ease of access to such minor adjustments as the amount of momentum and the minimum and maximum output voltage.

These adjustments are not essential. The simplest transistor throttle in this book, in fact, uses only two absolutely essential controls, speed and direction. A throttle designed with a number of adjustments always can be simplified to these two basic functions, with possibly a brake in addition. The reduction in flexibility is small.

**What is pulse operation?** Nearly all model locomotive motors operate on direct current. Smooth, filtered d.c. is a continuous unmodulated voltage, such as a battery supplies. This constant voltage is ideal for running trains because there is a minimum of motor heating and brush sparking, but filtered d.c. is not so good for starting slowly and smoothly. For starts, nearly all transistor throttles use pulsed d.c. The current is interrupted between 30 and 120 times a second. This rapid interruption vibrates the motor armature, loosening sticky bearings, gears, and rods, and makes possible smooth jerk-free starts.

Most transistor throttles use the 60-hertz a.c. present at the throttle input as a pulse source. A few, such as Linn Westcott's TAT IV, derive their pulses from internal oscillator circuits.

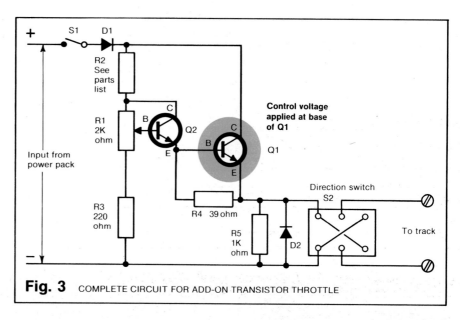

**Fig. 3**  COMPLETE CIRCUIT FOR ADD-ON TRANSISTOR THROTTLE

Ideally, the pulse of a transistor throttle should disappear automatically at higher running speeds to avoid motor overheating. One way to tell if pulse is present at high speeds is to notice if the locomotive headlight is excessively bright.

**What is momentum or flywheel effect?** When the engineer opens the throttle of the prototype there always is a delay until speed picks up, particularly if hundreds of tons are coupled to the drawbar. The same is true when braking: A speeding freight usually takes a mile or more to come to a standstill. Neither the pound or two our trains weigh nor the high-ratio worm drive contribute to coasting and slow starting, and a flywheel often is impractical because of space restrictions. Therefore inertia must be simulated electronically.

When you turn up a throttle with an inertia or momentum simulator or operate the brake, a simple delay circuit, using a resistor and a capacitor, slows the rate of change of the track voltage.

Most transistor throttles have a switch on the front panel to cut out the delay circuit. For yard work and switching moves, most modelers prefer fast-acting throttles and brakes, and they cut in the momentum effect once the train is made up and on the main line.

**Does a transistor throttle wear out?** A well-designed and protected throttle is durable and lasts many years. Most transistor throttles use two electrolytic capacitors. These tend to lose capacity if they are unused over a period of time, but they also regain capacity after use. If you have a transistor throttle that worked well when you last used it several months ago but now has a low output or almost no momentum effect, leave it running for an hour or so and it will likely rejuvenate itself.

By the way, any smoke or unpleasant or odd smell from a throttle, transistor or not, means damage, so pull the plug immediately.

**Can two transistor throttles be powered from one transformer?** Not if you use the common-rail system of dividing the layout into blocks. You would have a direct short through the common rail if the two throttles were switched in opposite directions. Even if you do not use common rail, a good idea is to use a separate transformer for each throttle. Otherwise a heavy load on one throttle would affect the output of any other throttle using the same transformer.

**Can transistor throttles be used for walkaround controls?** A walkaround control is a handheld unit used on larger layouts to allow the operator to follow a train around the layout for on-the-spot control. Connection to the layout is through long wires which must be heavy enough to carry the full motor current. With a transistor or SCR throttle, the speed control carries only a low current, so it is a simple matter to bring three wires and the small potentiometer outside the throttle case on an extension cable, using light flexible wires.

To arrange for remote reversing, the problem arises that any extension reversing switch must carry the full motor current, putting us right back where we started, with heavy leads. The reversing switch must be replaced with a 2-pole relay operated with the d.c. available across the speed control and switched with a button on the walkaround unit. This requires only one more wire through the cable. Fig. 4 shows a schematic that can be applied to all the throttles in this book.

## Add-on transistor throttle

Many model railroaders avoid transistor throttles because of their cost and complexity. The add-on miniature transistor throttle is simple in design and costs less than $10 to build. It operates from the d.c. output of your power pack.

If you've never built a transistor circuit before, this simple circuit should encourage you. Many of the parts can be

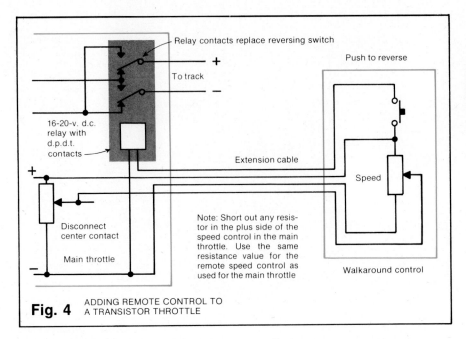

Relay contacts replace reversing switch

Push to reverse

To track

+

−

16-20-v. d.c. relay with d.p.d.t. contacts

Extension cable

Speed

+

Disconnect center contact

Main throttle

Note: Short out any resistor in the plus side of the speed control in the main throttle. Use the same resistance value for the remote speed control as used for the main throttle

Walkaround control

−

**Fig. 4**  ADDING REMOTE CONTROL TO A TRANSISTOR THROTTLE

Fig. 5 (above) and Fig. 6 (below). The interior and exterior views of the add-on transistor throttle show how simple the construction of the device is. Note the piece of aluminum that serves as a heat sink.

used to construct the more complicated throttles described later. This version is for N and HO, but if your motors draw more than 1 amp or you want to operate double-headers, then choose one of the more powerful designs in this book.

Although this miniature transistor throttle lacks many of the features of more exotic throttles, such as momentum circuitry and a brake control, it does offer the two biggest advantages of transistor throttles: smooth starts and smooth adjustment of running speed.

**Throttle rating:** Most transistor throttles use three transistors; why does the add-on throttle use only two? By specifying that this throttle be used only with N or HO trains, the maximum current requirement of this throttle is limited to what can be handled by two transistors, about .5 to 1 amp.

One caution: Power packs for N scale trains with less than a 10-volt-amp rating may not be satisfactory for use with a transistor throttle because of lost voltage. Check the rating plate of the power pack.

"Lost voltage" refers to the reduced output compared to the input voltage. Each device in the control chain loses a little voltage because of the amount of voltage required to turn it on. This throttle loses about 3 volts; in other words, if 16 volts goes in, 13 volts comes out. This loss is not really a handicap, because most locomotives run at somewhat more than top scale speed at full voltage.

**Construction:** Figs. 5 and 6 show the completed throttle, inside and out. Positioning of the parts inside the case is not critical, and there are so few parts that a printed circuit board isn't worthwhile. Figs. 7, 8, and 9 show the wiring step by step, with new wiring added at each step shown in color. Fig. 10 shows the full wiring layout.

The easiest way to wire is to start at the outside and work in. Center-punch

and drill the holes for the potentiometer, the switch, the input leads, and the screws for mounting the terminal strip and the heat sink. Drill all these holes in the top and ends of the case, so the bottom and sides are free of all wires and parts, making the case easier to take apart. You may substitute a second terminal strip for the input leads; be sure to mark which is which. All leads and connections should be insulated from the case.

Power transistor Q1 must be insulated from its metal heat sink. When you buy the transistor, ask for a TO-3-case mounting kit, which consists of two plastic bushings and a mica washer. A socket to fit the transistor is available, but the mica washer still is needed for insulation. Mount the transistor as shown in fig. 16 of Chapter 2, and secure a soldering lug under one of the mounting nuts for making the collector connection.

The heat sink is a piece of sheet aluminum bent and mounted to the cabinet. The size isn't critical, but a thick piece, ⅛" or so, is preferable. It should have a flat surface for good thermal contact with the transistor. If the plastic

---

### PARTS FOR ADD-ON TRANSISTOR THROTTLE

| | |
|---|---|
| Q1 | NPN power transistor, such as 2N3055. |
| Q2 | NPN transistor with a 40-volt, .5-watt rating for N scale; for HO use a 40-volt, 1-watt high-gain transistor such as Texas Instrument TIS92. |
| S1 | See R1. |
| S2 | Dp.dt. toggle switch. |
| R1 | 2000-ohm carbon or wire-wound potentiometer with an off-on switch attached (S1). |
| R2 | 150-ohm, .5-watt carbon resistor for N; 39-ohm, .5-watt carbon resistor for HO. |
| R3 | 220-ohm, .5-watt carbon resistor. |
| R4 | 39-ohm, .5-watt carbon resistor. |
| R5 | 1000-ohm, .5-watt carbon resistor. |
| D1, D2 | 1-amp, 50-piv diodes. |
| Cabinet | 2½" x 3" x 5½", such as Bud CU2106A or Hammond (Canada) 1411N. |

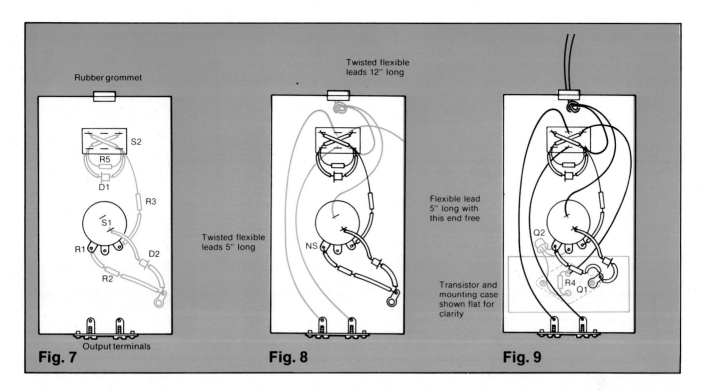

Fig. 7  Output terminals

Fig. 8

Fig. 9

Rubber grommet

Twisted flexible
leads 12" long

Twisted flexible
leads 5" long

Flexible lead
5" long with
this end free

Transistor and
mounting case
shown flat for
clarity

bushings are too long, preventing tight mounting, file them shorter.

When you drill the heat sink for the mounting screws for the transistor, also drill holes for the base and emitter leads, which must not touch the heat sink. Before you mount the transistor, note somewhere which lead — base, emitter, and collector — is which. Commercial heat sinks are available; if you use one, make sure it fits inside the case.

Use a rubber grommet for the input leads to prevent chafing of the wire against the case. Tie a knot in the leads inside the case to prevent them from being pulled from their soldered connections. (Since the wires are thinner and more flexible and the voltages and currents are lower, knotting the leads is not the bad practice it would be with a line cord carrying 115-volt a.c.)

Be careful to connect the diodes with correct polarity.

**Testing and operation:** Double-check your wiring against fig. 10, and make sure all your soldered connections are good. Connect the input leads of the throttle to the d.c. terminals of your power pack, connect the output leads to the track, and turn the throttle of the power pack all the way on. If the locomotive doesn't run, flip the reversing switch of the power pack.

The transistor throttle control knob operates much like the power pack rheostat, except for its improved speed control. The control knob has an off-on switch that shuts off the output voltage entirely when the knob is turned to the extreme counterclockwise position. When the switch is turned on, the output voltage jumps to about 2 volts. This reduces the dead space when turning the control knob up from zero to the starting voltage.

You now have the most basic transistor throttle. Its action is smoother than an ordinary train-set power pack. The speed control itself, with a 320-degree range of adjustment, offers a better feeling for control than the simple slide control of most train-set power packs.

### SCR throttle

Just two switches and two pushbuttons are the controls for this silicon-controlled-rectifier throttle. The main control is a center-off switch, spring-loaded to the off position. Flip it one way and the train gradually builds up speed; flip it the other and the train progressively brakes. If you flip the switch briefly one way or the other, the train accelerates or brakes and stays at the new speed when the switch is returned to the center position. Simulating the notches of the prototype's throttle and brake is easy.

One of the other controls is the conventional reversing switch, one pushbutton is for panic stops, and the other, called the pulse peaker, is good for dirt-busting — moving a balky locomotive. When pressed, the pulse peaker supplies full voltage until released, regardless of the position of the throttle-brake control.

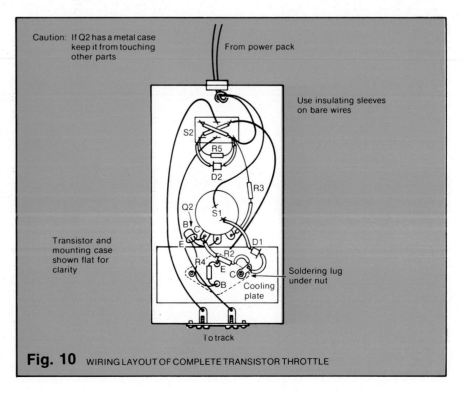

Caution: If Q2 has a metal case keep it from touching other parts

From power pack

Use insulating sleeves on bare wires

Transistor and mounting case shown flat for clarity

Soldering lug under nut

Cooling plate

To track

**Fig. 10**  WIRING LAYOUT OF COMPLETE TRANSISTOR THROTTLE

This SCR throttle also has automatic voltage feedback: The power to the rails increases and decreases with changes in the load, helping the train maintain a constant speed.

**The SCR circuit:** The speed-controlling element in this throttle is a silicon controlled rectifier (SCR). It looks like a stud-type rectifier. The extra lead is a gate connection which is used to switch on the diode part of the SCR. If voltage is applied to the diode section, the SCR doesn't conduct in either direction, but if the gate is made just a little positive compared with the cathode, the SCR acts like a diode and passes current in one direction.

Once the diode is turned on by the gate, it can't be shut off by reversing the process — making the gate negative. The whole supply must be shut down before the SCR turns off. If alternating voltage is applied, as from a power transformer, then the supply to the SCR shuts down 60 times a second.

In this circuit the gate is triggered every time the anode of the SCR is positive with respect to its cathode, so the SCR output contains positive pulses at a frequency of 60 hertz. These pulses are satisfactory for driving permanent-magnet model motors.

The speed control determines how early in each pulse of positive a.c. the SCR turns on. Since the SCR doesn't turn off until each pulse of voltage collapses to zero before swinging negative, the earlier the gate turns the SCR on, the higher the energy which comes through the SCR diode to run the motor. If the

gate turns the SCR on late in the positive voltage cycle, then the output is low and the motor runs slowly. The SCR acts like a switch, not a resistance, and it does not produce as much heat as a transistor does.

Because the SCR is turned off half the time (when the a.c. input is negative) it requires a higher input voltage than a transistor to maintain the same voltage to the track. Although this circuit is designed to operate on 20 volts, it can use 16 volts at the cost of a reduced maximum speed.

Referring to the circuit in fig. 12, transistor Q3 determines the time the SCR is turned on: Both d.c. and a.c. signals are on Q3 input. The d.c. can be turned up or down by the throttle-brake switch to boost the a.c. signal or suppress it.

The a.c. signal is coupled via C3 and Q1; the d.c. signal is coupled via Q2 and momentum capacitor C2.

Diode D1 rectifies the a.c. input, and C1 is used as a filter capacitor. These components provide filtered d.c. for the transistors. Diode D2 suppresses any pulses that might be sent back into the throttle from some external source. These could damage C6, which is used to shape the pulse output of the throttle to reduce any motor overheating effects that might occur. C6 in particular must be a high-quality component, since it passes high currents at full output. This is one reason for specifying at least a 100-volt component here, even though only about 25 volts peak are applied across it.

Fig. 11. The SCR throttle has a lever switch to increase and decrease train speed. Although the lever is quite different from the usual rheostat knob, it is easy to use.

**Overload indicator:** Lamp L1, connected in one of the output leads, is used not only to indicate overload, but also to protect the throttle from the damage that could be caused by continuous short circuits in the track or motor. A 2-amp, 12-volt lamp ensures that at the full normal output current for the pack, up to 1 amp, the lamp glows dimly, if at all. However, if the output of the pack accidentally is shorted, the lamp lights to partial or full brightness. It effectively acts as a buffer

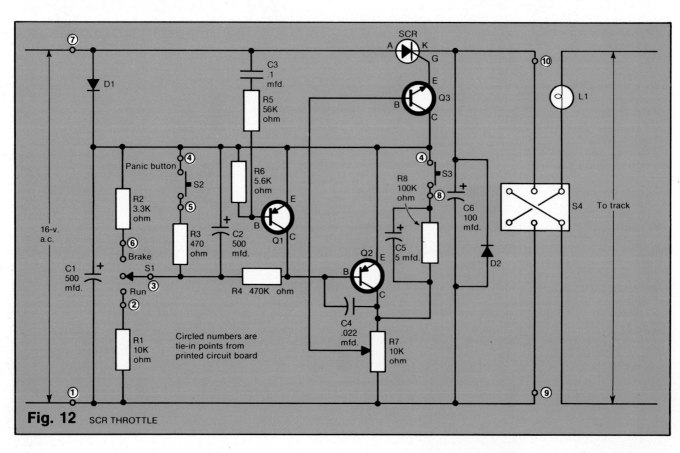

**Fig. 12** SCR THROTTLE

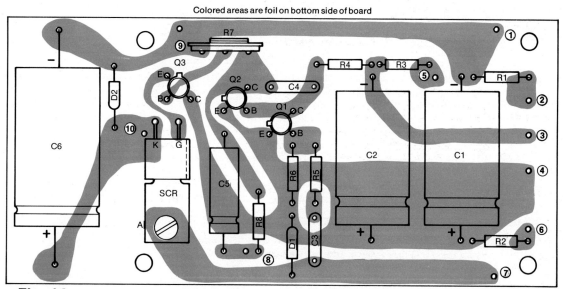

Shown with foil side up

**Fig. 13** FULL SIZE TEMPLATE FOR SCR THROTTLE

Colored areas are foil on bottom side of board

**Fig. 14** COMPONENT LAYOUT OF SCR THROTTLE

between the SCR and the short circuit, eliminating any chance of damage.

The lamp's resistance is low, less than an ohm, when its filament is cold, and it does not interfere with the operation of the train under normal conditions. However, when the output current rises drastically, the lamp lights and the filament resistance increases to 5 or 6 ohms. This resistance, being between the throttle and the external short, limits the short-circuit current to a safe 2 amps. When the lamp lights, press the "panic" button to stop the train and then pull the line voltage plug until you've corrected the problem.

**Construction:** The SCR throttle is illustrated for printed circuit board assembly. The PC board makes the unit easy to duplicate, for once you've made one printed-wiring throttle, you can use it as a guide for assembling others (after making sure the first one works, of course). A printed circuit board is not

mandatory, of course. Wiring of this type of throttle is not critical. If you want to assemble this design using tag-boards and connecting wire, go ahead — you will have no problems.

Fig. 13 is a full-size printed board layout, with the copper areas in white. Use this diagram as a master to cut your own negative, as detailed in Chapter 1. Remember to remove the film over the white areas only. Use a mapping pen and India ink to mark the centers of the holes for the component wires. When the board is made, the hole centers will show as uncoppered dots.

Clean the remaining copper area with a household cleanser or fine steel wool so the solder will adhere properly.

Fig. 14 shows, full size, which components go where. The copper foil layout is ghosted in for guidance purposes. To mount the components, push the leads through the board and bend them over slightly to hold the compo-

nent in place. Solder the lead to the copper area of the board, and then trim the excess length of the wire. Be careful to solder all the leads on the copper side of the board. There are nearly 50 solder connections to make, and it is easy to miss one.

To connect the board assembly to the power source and the panel controls, plug the 10 holes in the board with short pieces of copper wire and solder the wires to the copper area of the board. Then solder the leads to the pieces of wire that protrude from the component side of the board. Hole numbers and corresponding connections are:

| 1, 7 | a.c. input |
|------|------------|
| 2 | "run" side of throttle lever switch |
| 3 | center pole of throttle |
| 4 | one side of both buttons |
| 5 | panic button |
| 6 | "brake" side of throttle |
| 8 | pulse peaker button |
| 9, 10 | center poles of reverse switch |

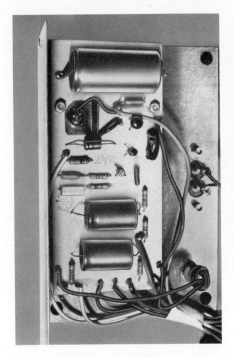

Fig. 15. The use of a printed circuit board in the construction of the SCR throttle results in a neat and sturdy unit.

Fig. 17. The connections to the two pushbuttons, the speed control, the direction switch, and the lamp appear in this view of the inside of the SCR throttle. Be sure to leave enough slack in the wiring so the two halves of the case can be taken apart.

Be sure to allow enough length in the connecting leads so you can open the case for adjustments and repairs.

Fig. 11 shows the arrangement of the control panel. The exact location of the controls is not critical, but space the controls far enough apart so the wires to them are not likely to tangle and short or get in the way of your soldering iron when you are working on the adjacent component.

The lever switch in the photograph is a Centralab switch, No. 1455. It requires two holes 1⅝" apart plus a slot ⅛" wide and 1¼" long between the two holes. Make the slot by drilling a series of ⅛" holes and then filing the slot clean.

The terminal strip requires two holes for mounting screws and a larger hole or a slot for the backs of the terminals. Be sure the hole for the input leads is protected with a rubber grommet, and knot the leads on the inside of the case. Mount the printed circuit board to the bottom of the case using spacers or metal support brackets at the corners. Don't let the mounting screws touch any of the copper area of the board.

Mount the power transformer in a separate cabinet, following the safety precautions mentioned in Chapter 1.

Canadian hobbyists using the Hammond transformer will notice an extra center-tap lead in the secondary winding. Insulate it, since it isn't used. The Hammond transformer is actually a 20-volt type. Any transformer rated at 1 amp and 16 to 20 volts can be used because of the range of the voltage set-up resistor, R7.

**Adjustment:** Carbon potentiometer R7 is a preset adjustment. The photographs show a miniature type designed for screwdriver adjustment. You also can use an ordinary shaft adjustment type, mounted on the back or sides of the cabinet.

Set the control so that at maximum output the locomotive lights are not excessively bright. Also check that locomotive motors are not overly hot after a prolonged run at full speed. If you have a hot-running motor, doubling the capacity of C6 to 200 mfd. probably will cure the problem.

As a final test, check that the overload indicator glows when the output is

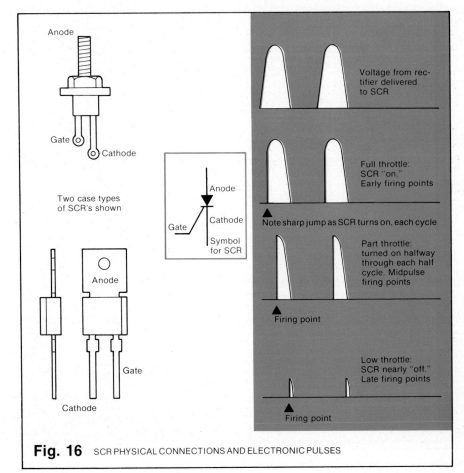

**Fig. 16** SCR PHYSICAL CONNECTIONS AND ELECTRONIC PULSES

shorted and the throttle switch is held at maximum speed.

### High-capacity throttle

The simple transistor throttle described in the first part of this chapter has a limited capacity, suitable only for N scale or small HO scale locomotives. For higher currents another transistor must be added to the circuit.

When momentum effect and a brake control are added, the throttle must operate from filtered d.c., because no matter where in the circuit the momentum storage capacitor is placed it removes the d.c. pulses on which the throttle operates.

Because of these requirements the throttle described in this section is considerably more complicated than the preceding ones. In order that it can be built in stages, the brake and momentum unit is in a separate plug-in box; the throttle can operate without it.

Changes in component specifications make this design suitable for 1-, 2-, or 3-amp output currents. See the parts list and select components for your throttle accordingly.

**Operating features:** Without the brake and momentum unit the throttle provides the usual fast response to changes in the setting of the control knob. When the brake and momentum unit is added, train speed responds very

gradually to changes in the throttle setting, very much like the prototype. A spring-loaded switch gives the option of either heavy or light braking. When the switch is held in either position the train

slows to a full stop, regardless of the throttle position. When the brake is released the train picks up speed gradually to a level corresponding with the throttle setting.

## PARTS FOR SCR THROTTLE

| | |
|---|---|
| D1, D2 | 1-amp, 200-piv diodes. |
| Q1, Q2 | PNP small-signal silicon transistor with a 40-volt, .5-watt rating, such as 2N2907 or 2N2696. |
| Q3 | NPN small-signal silicon transistor with a 40-volt, .5-watt rating. |
| SCR | Silicon controlled rectifier rated for at least 100 volts and 3 amps average current, such as Transitron TCR18 or G.E. 2N1772. |
| S1 | Sp.dt. spring-loaded center-off switch, such as Centralab 1453 or 1455. |
| S2, S4 | Sp.st. pushbutton, such as Switchcraft type 101 or 201. |
| S3 | Dp.dt. toggle switch. |
| R1 | 10,000-ohm, .5-watt carbon resistor. |
| R2 | 3300-ohm, .5-watt carbon resistor. |
| R3 | 470-ohm, .5-watt carbon resistor. |
| R4 | 470,000-ohm, .5-watt carbon resistor. |
| R5 | 56,000-ohm, .5-watt carbon resistor. |
| R6 | 5600-ohm, .5-watt carbon resistor. |
| R7 | 10,000-ohm carbon potentiometer. |
| R8 | 100,000-ohm, .5-watt carbon resistor. |
| C1, C2 | 500-mfd., 50-wvdc electrolytic capacitors. |
| C3 | .1-mfd., 100-wvdc paper or polyester capacitor. |
| C4 | .022-mfd., 100-wvdc paper or polyester capacitor. |
| C5 | 5-mfd., 50-wvdc electrolytic capacitor. |
| C6 | 100-mfd., 100-wvdc electrolytic capacitor. |
| T1 | 18-volt, 1-amp power transformer, such as Chicago-Stancor TP-1 or Hammond (Canada) 166J20. |
| L1 | 12-volt, 2-amp (or 32-candlepower) lamp. |
| F1 | .5-amp fuse in Buss HJM fuseholder. |
| Cabinet | 3″ x 5″ x 7″, such as Bud CU2108A or Hammond (Canada) 1411Q. |

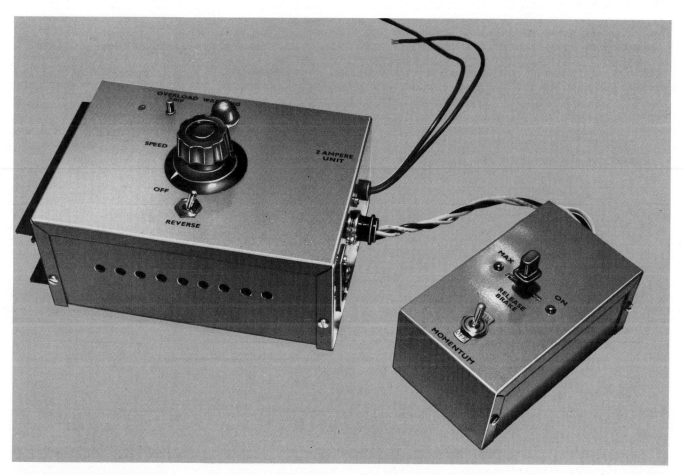

Fig. 18. This is the 2-amp version of the high-capacity throttle. The cabinet on the left contains the speed control, the reversing switch, and the protection devices. The small plug-in unit, which can be added later, contains the brake and momentum circuitry.

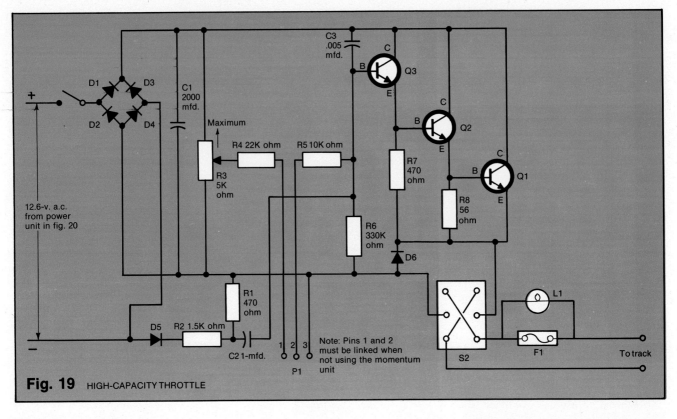

**Fig. 19** HIGH-CAPACITY THROTTLE

Labels within Fig. 19:
- 12.6-v. a.c. from power unit in fig. 20
- D1, D3, D2, D4
- C1 2000 mfd.
- C3 .005 mfd.
- Q3, Q2, Q1 (C, B, E on each)
- Maximum
- R4 22K ohm
- R5 10K ohm
- R3 5K ohm
- R7 470 ohm
- R8 56 ohm
- R6 330K ohm
- D6
- R1 470 ohm
- D5
- R2 1.5K ohm
- C2 1-mfd.
- 1 2 3 / P1
- Note: Pins 1 and 2 must be linked when not using the momentum unit
- S2
- L1
- F1
- To track

## PARTS FOR HIGH-CAPACITY THROTTLE

| | |
|---|---|
| D1-D4 | 200-piv, 1-amp silicon diodes (for 3-amp version use 2-amp silicon diodes). |
| D5 | 200-piv silicon or germanium diode (current rating is unimportant). |
| D6 | 200-piv, 1-amp silicon diode. |
| Q1 | NPN silicon power transistor with a 40-volt, 15-amp rating, such as 2N3055. |
| Q2 | NPN silicon transistor with a 40-volt, 1-amp, 1-watt rating such as 2N5856 or 2N3053. |
| Q3 | NPN silicon transistor with a 40-volt, .2-amp, .3-watt rating such as SE4021 or 2N4248. |
| C1 | 1000-mfd., 25-wvdc electrolytic capacitor for the 1-amp throttle; 2000-mfd., 25-wvdc electrolytic capacitor for the 2-amp and 3-amp throttles. Use a capacitor with axial leads. A mounting clip for the capacitor makes construction easier. |
| C2 | 1-mfd., 100-wvdc polyester or paper (not electrolytic) capacitor. |
| C3 | .005-mfd. ceramic disk capacitor. |
| R1 | 470-ohm, .5-watt carbon resistor. |
| R2 | 1500-ohm, .5-watt carbon resistor. |
| R3 | 5000-ohm linear carbon potentiometer with sp.st. switch (S1). |
| R4 | 22,000-ohm, .5-watt carbon resistor. |
| R5 | 10,000-ohm, .5-watt carbon resistor. |
| R6 | 330,000-ohm, .5-watt carbon resistor. |
| R7 | 470-ohm, .5-watt carbon resistor. |
| R8 | 56-ohm, .5-watt carbon resistor. |
| S1 | See R3. |
| S2 | Dp.dt. toggle switch. |
| F1 | Manually-resettable thermal circuit breaker, such as Mallory CBB-100, CBB-200, and CBB-300, for the 1-amp, 2-amp, and 3-amp throttles respectively. |
| L1 | No. 53 lamp (14.4-volt) in Dialco holder, or the equivalent. |
| Heat sink | Wakefield Delta-T NC401A for the 2-amp throttle; NC403A for the 3-amp throttle. |
| Cabinet | 3″ x 5″ x 7″, such as Bud CU2108A or Hammond (Canada) 1411Q. |
| P1 | 3-prong plug and socket, such as Amphenol 71-3S and 78-S3S. |
| Transformer | 1-amp: Chicago-Stancor P8384 or Hammond (Canada) 166J12. 2-amp: Chicago-Stancor P8130 or Hammond (Canada) 167L12. 3-amp: Chicago-Stancor P8358 or Hammond (Canada) 167N12. You will need terminal strips, knobs, and other assorted hardware. |

**The circuit:** This throttle (fig. 19) requires 12.6-volt a.c. input, derived from a separate power transformer. (There is no electrical reason why the transformer can't be in the cabinet with the throttle. Mechanically, however, such placement would result in an awkwardly large cabinet that would have to be much stronger because of the weight of the transformer.)

Diodes D1, D2, D3, and D4 form a bridge rectifier. Together with the filter capacitor, C1, they convert the 12.6-volt a.c. input to about 16-volt d.c. Variable potentiometer R1 is the throttle speed control, and off-on switch S1 is ganged to it. Resistor R4 assists in short-circuit protection, and when the brake and momentum unit is coupled, it is also part of the momentum-simulating circuit.

Transistor Q1 is the voltage-regulating transistor. Transistors Q2 and Q3 perform the current amplification necessary to transform the small control currents through R3 and R4 up to the large motor currents through Q1.

Diode D6 protects the throttle from the accidental connection of external voltage and also suppresses any pulses

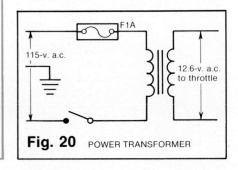

**Fig. 20** POWER TRANSFORMER

Labels within Fig. 20:
- F1A
- 115-v. a.c.
- 12.6-v. a.c. to throttle

28

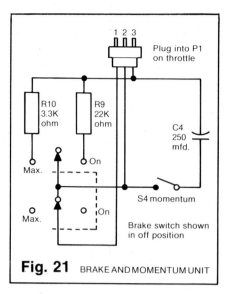

**Fig. 21** BRAKE AND MOMENTUM UNIT

(In figure 21:)
- 1 2 3 — Plug into P1 on throttle
- R10 3.3K ohm
- R9 22K ohm
- C4 250 mfd.
- Max. / On
- Max. / On
- S4 momentum
- Brake switch shown in off position

Fig. 22. The brake unit consists of two switches, two resistors, and a capacitor.

**PARTS FOR BRAKE AND MOMENTUM UNIT**

| | |
|---|---|
| R9 | 22,000-ohm, .5-watt carbon resistor. |
| R10 | 3300-ohm, .5-watt carbon resistor. |
| C4 | 250-mfd., 25-wvdc electrolytic capacitor. |
| S3 | Dp.dt. spring-loaded center-off switch, such as Centralab 1453 or 1455. |
| S4 | Sp.st. toggle switch. |
| Cabinet | 2⅛″ x 3″ x 5¼″, such as Bud CU2106A or Hammond (Canada) 1411N. |

from the motor that might arrive at Q1.

Circuit breaker F1 is essential for the 2-amp and 3-amp versions of this throttle. It consists of an enclosed spring-loaded heating element which disconnects the load automatically should the throttle be overloaded. When tripped, the device must be reset by pushing in a button on the control panel. To indicate that the overload trip has operated but the external short still is present, lamp L1 lights. When the short is cleared the lamp goes out and the trip may be reset. Remove locomotives from the track when you search for overloads, because L1 also senses them when the overload trip operates.

**Pulse:** Since the throttle operates on filtered d.c., the pulses necessary for slow running and smooth starts must be injected at some stage. Diode D5 allows positive half cycles of input a.c. to pass through R1 and R2, which reduce the amplitude, and C2, which blocks d.c., to the base of Q3. As a result, 60-hertz pulses are present in the output at a sufficient level to overcome "stiction" without causing motor overheating.

**Brake and momentum unit:** Fig. 21 shows the circuit of the add-on brake and momentum unit. Capacitor C4 stores energy when the throttle control is turned down and takes time to recharge when the throttle is turned up — like an electrical sponge. This capacitor can be disconnected with switch S4. Resistors R9 and R10 are used to leak charge from the capacitor, acting as braking-rate devices. The lower the resistance the faster the charge leakage and the faster the braking action. Brake switch S3 disconnects the throttle control voltage when the "brakes" are applied. The control voltage is automatically reapplied progressively when the brakes are released.

When the brake and momentum unit isn't used, pins 1 and 2 of socket P1 on

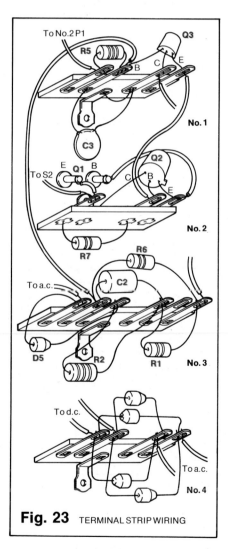

**Fig. 23** TERMINAL STRIP WIRING

(Labels in figure 23:)
- To No.2 P1
- R5
- Q3 — B C E
- C3
- No. 1
- To S2
- E Q1 B
- Q2 — C B E
- No. 2
- R6
- R7
- C2
- To a.c.
- D5
- R2
- R1
- No. 3
- To d.c.
- To a.c.
- No. 4

the throttle unit must be joined. The easiest way to do this is with a plug that fits into the socket on the throttle unit. Simply run a short jumper wire between the proper pins.

**Construction:** Fig. 24 shows the component layout of the 1-amp and 2-amp

throttles. Power transistor Q1 is secured to one side of the outside of the cabinet. For the 1-amp throttle, remove the paint from the transistor mounting area to ensure good thermal contact. Use paint remover and a cloth; don't use an abrasive. Mount the transistor with the usual mica washer, plastic bushings, and thermally conductive silicone grease. For the 2-amp throttle, mount the transistor with a cast aluminum heat sink secured to the outside of the cabinet to permit the heat to be dissipated. The cabinet itself will become warm to the touch after use. For the 3-amp variation, quite a large heat sink is necessary. Mount it on the removable back of the cabinet, and connect Q1 to the rest of the circuit with three flexible leads.

Mount the cabinet so that cooling air can flow past the fins of the heat sinks. Never mount these throttles in a place where air flow is restricted.

Note that most of the small components are mounted on four tagboards. Their assembly is sketched in fig. 23.

Bring the input leads through a rubber grommet on one side of the case, and knot the leads inside for strain relief. The output terminals and the plug for the brake and momentum unit can be mounted on that same side of the cabinet.

The front panel contains the speed control, the direction toggle switch, the overload indicator lamp, and the overload reset button. Drill a row of ¼″ holes in each side of the cabinet for ventilation.

Construction of the separate momentum unit is straightforward. Drill the holes for the toggle switch and the brake lever, and file a slot for the lever. Anchor the common leads for R9, R10, and C4 and lead 3 from the plug to a single-lug tie strip mounted on the back of the cabinet. Feed the leads from the plug to the cabinet, knot them inside the cabinet, and connect the ends to the tie strip and the proper contacts on S3 (fig. 24).

**Variations:** The 1-amp, 2-amp, and 3-amp throttles vary in several of the components.

Diodes D1-D4: For the 1-amp and 2-amp throttles use 1-amp diodes. For the 3-amp throttle use 1.5-amp or 2-amp diodes, or use two 1-amp diodes in parallel for each arm of the bridge. The 2-amp diodes may have to be assembled on a piece of insulating board, since most diodes that size are secured by a threaded stud and a nut.

Power transistor heat sink and tagboards 1 and 2: For the 1-amp and 2-amp throttles, tagboards 1 and 2 are secured by the nuts used to fasten power transistor Q1 to the side of the cabinet. The securing lug for each tagboard is used as the collector connection for Q1, because the nut, though insulated from the cabinet, is connected through the screw to the transistor case. For the 3-amp throttle, tagboards 1 and 2 need another lug for connection to the case of Q1.

Circuit breaker: This is available with the appropriate rating for the output. It is not essential for the 1-amp version and can be omitted, along with the warning lamp, because the higher resistance of the 1-amp power transformer limits the short-circuit current available.

Filter capacitor C1: Use a 1000-mfd. device for the 1-amp throttle; 2000-mfd. for the 2-amp and 3-amp throttles.

Driver transistor Q2: If you use the Philips BFY52 and you are building the 3-amp throttle, add a TO-5 heat sink.

**Testing:** Carefully check the polarity of all diodes and electrolytic capacitors. Make sure the base and emitter connections of Q1 have not been transposed accidentally and the connections to Q2 and Q3 are correct, especially if you have substituted components. Not all transistors have leads arranged in the same pattern.

Test the overload trip by short-circuiting the output terminals briefly with a screwdriver. The trip should operate and light the lamp within 3 or 4 seconds at all positions of the speed control.

**Operating:** Don't be tempted to feed in more than 12.6 volts a.c. The low-load output of this throttle is about 15 volts d.c., and full-load output is about 10 volts d.c. This voltage produces full speed with almost any locomotive. A higher input voltage adds nothing in power or realism, but it increases the heat to be dissipated by the transistors.

For yard work, where a fast throttle response is required, switch off the momentum effect. For longer runs on the layout, switch in the momentum and use the brake lever to control speeds and bring the train to a stop.

## Full-feature throttle

The full-feature design is suitable for all HO and N scale applications. It provides train control that is very close to prototype operation. It has a brake handle with five positions labeled for the positions of the prototype brake and performing the same operations (fig. 25).

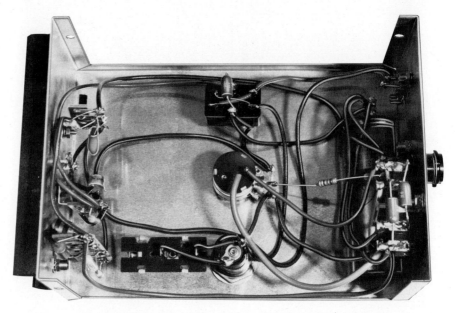

Fig. 24. Most of the components of the high-capacity throttle are mounted on tag strips. The wire leads of the components are stiff enough to hold the components in position. At the left on the outside of the cabinet is the heat sink for the main transistor.

### PARTS FOR FULL-FEATURE THROTTLE

| | |
|---|---|
| Q1 | NPN silicon power transistor, such as 2N3055. |
| Q2 | NPN silicon transistor, such as Fairchild SE8002 or BFY52 (Canada). |
| Q3 | NPN silicon transistor, such as Fairchild SE2002 or BC107 (Canada). |
| D1-D4 | 1-amp, 200-piv diodes. |
| D5 | 16-volt, 250-mw. zener diode, such as 1N720A or BZY88/C16 (Canada). |
| D6-D8, D10, D11 | General-purpose 40-piv germanium diodes, such as 1N541, 1N617, or 1N618. |
| D9 | 1-amp, 200-piv diode. |
| T1 | 12.6-volt, 2-amp power transformer, such as Chicago-Stancor P8130 or Hammond (Canada) 167L12. |
| F1 | 1-amp, fast-blow, panel-mounting fuse and fuseholder, such as Buss HSM. |
| F2 | 2-amp thermal circuit breaker, such as Mallory CBB-200. |
| S1 | 2p.5t. rotary switch, such as Centralab CRL 1002 or CRL 1404. |
| S2 | Sp.dt. slide switch, such as Stackpole SS-26-1. |
| S3 | Dp.dt. center-off toggle switch. |
| L1, L2 | No. 53 lamps and holders. |
| R1 | 150-ohm, .5-watt carbon resistor. |
| R2 | 2000-ohm, .5-watt carbon potentiometer, rear section, such as IRC M11-110. R2 is ganged with R14. |
| R3 | 220-ohm, .5-watt carbon resistor. |
| R4 | 22,000-ohm, .5-watt carbon resistor. |
| R5 | 22,000-ohm, .5-watt carbon resistor. |
| R6 | 1000-ohm, .5-watt carbon resistor. |
| R7 | 10,000-ohm, .5-watt carbon resistor. |
| R8 | 470,000-ohm, .5-watt carbon resistor. |
| R9 | 1000-ohm, 1-watt carbon resistor. |
| R10 | 39-ohm, .5-watt carbon resistor. |
| R11 | 3300-ohm, .5-watt carbon resistor. |
| R12 | 6800-ohm, .5-watt carbon resistor. |
| R13 | 1000-ohm, .5-watt carbon resistor. |
| R14 | 2000-ohm, .5-watt carbon potentiometer, front section, such as IRC PQ11-110. R14 is ganged with R2. |
| R25 | 4700-ohm, .5-watt carbon resistor. |
| R26 | 100,000-ohm, .5-watt carbon resistor (needed only if neon lamp NE does not have a built-in resistor). |
| C1 | 2000-mfd., 25-wvdc electrolytic capacitor and clip, such as Sprague 39D. |
| C2 | 250-mfd., 25-wvdc electrolytic capacitor, such as Mallory TC25025. |
| C3 | .01-mfd., 100-wvdc ceramic disk or paper capacitor. |
| NE | Neon lamp and holder, such as Leecraft 36N-2311. |
| Ch1 | Make 200 turns of No. 16 enameled copper wire on a 1"-diameter form. |
| Cabinet | 4" x 7" x 12", such as Bud CU2111A or Hammond (Canada) 1411X. |
| Cabinet | Optional for the transformer enclosure. Bud CU2106A and Hammond (Canada) 1411N are both suitable. |

Fig. 25. The panel of the full-feature throttle includes a speed control, a five-position brake knob, switches for direction and momentum, a horn button, and three indicator lights.

**Brake positions:** The brake has five positions: Release, Lap, Service, Quick Service, and Emergency. Release, as its name implies, releases all brake action. This is the normal position for starts and yard operation.

In the Lap position, the speed attained by opening the throttle is maintained for some time but the train eventually coasts to a stop. This position is useful for run-

ning, using Quick Service (one notch clockwise, to slow the train for curves), and Release (one notch counter-clockwise, for resuming speed).

Service is a gentle braking position and Quick Service is a fairly hard brake application.

Emergency stops the train almost on a dime. The brake has faster action than prototype emergency, but keeping your

brass articulated out of that open draw-bridge takes precedence over prototype braking action.

**Pulse generator:** For smooth low-speed operation of model motors the voltage must be applied in pulses. The best pulse rate is about 40 hertz. The pulses should be rectangular in shape, and each pulse should last about 2.5 milliseconds, according to Linn West-cott, editor of MODEL RAILROADER. These specifications are the best compromise for performance with minimum noise from the motor.

Thus far in this book all the throttles have had pulse operation derived from the 60-hertz house current. However, even after this pulse has been shaped and clipped electronically, it's still not the optimum, though it is better than no pulse at all.

The design outlined on these pages uses a special three-transistor circuit to generate 40-hertz pulses. An extra control is ganged with the throttle control to make the pulses maximum at low throttle and disappear completely at high-speed settings. As an extra touch, a pre-set control is included for adjusting the width of the pulses, from about .7 milli-second to 10 milliseconds. Better-quality locomotives run well on the nar-row pulses; the wider pulses produce more noise but may be necessary for lo-

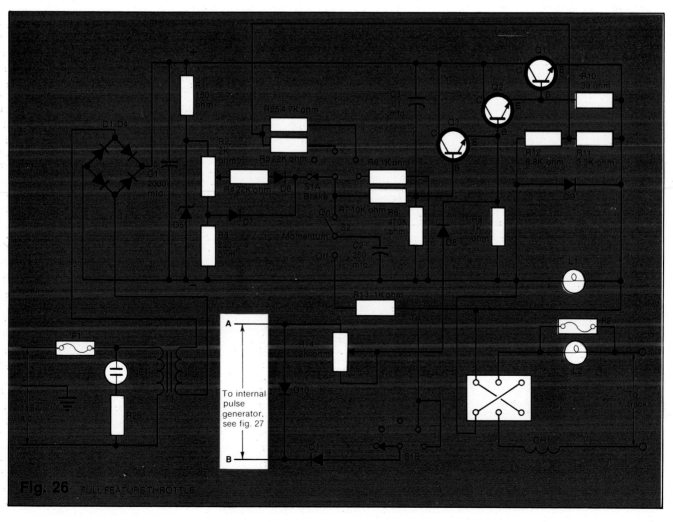

**Fig. 26** FULL-FEATURE THROTTLE

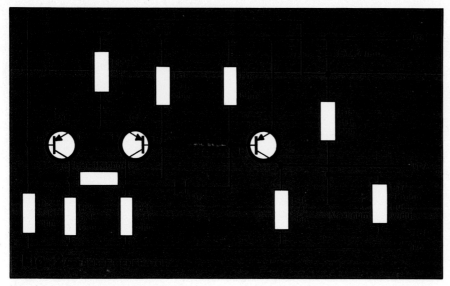

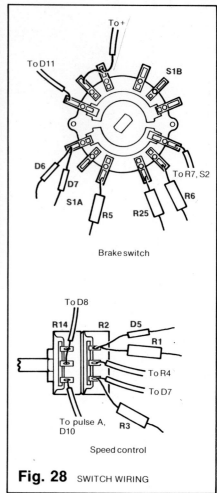

Brake switch

Speed control

**Fig. 28** SWITCH WIRING

comotives that look better than they run.

**Momentum effect:** A switch allows the momentum circuit to be operative for mainline running and turned off for yard work. The brake works very quickly in all braking positions when the momentum is switched off.

**Diesel horn:** A pushbutton controls an optional diesel horn. The horn sounds through a 4″ speaker which directs the sound back under the layout, tending to make the sound nondirectional.

The horn circuit is shown in Chapter 8. The horn uses the d.c. supply for power. The voltage is dropped to 9 volts by a resistor and a zener diode. The zener diode fixes the reduction so the pitch of the horn remains constant.

Location of the horn components is not critical. The horn button is within fingertip distance of the brake and throttle controls, and the pitch control is on the bottom of the cabinet.

**Other controls:** A small neon lamp remains lit while the unit is connected to the house current. Because this unit contains its own power transformer, for safety's sake never remove the cover while the unit is plugged in. The neon lamp serves as a warning.

A small incandescent lamp serves as an output voltage indicator, lighting brightly at full output and dimly at low voltages. In effect, it's a cheap voltmeter.

Another lamp is used as an overload indicator, lighting only when the overload trip has cut out and a heavy load or short circuit is in the layout. When the short is cleared the light goes out, indicating that the overload button may be reset.

The center-off type of direction switch has several advantages. The current to the track is switched off momentarily when changing direction, and the pulse voltage can be switched off when the lo-

comotive is stationary for a while. This throttle has maximum pulse at closed throttle, ideal for starting, but it causes some noise from a motor that is not yet turning. Keep the direction switch in the off position when the throttle is not in use, to isolate it from the track and to prevent damage if another live throttle

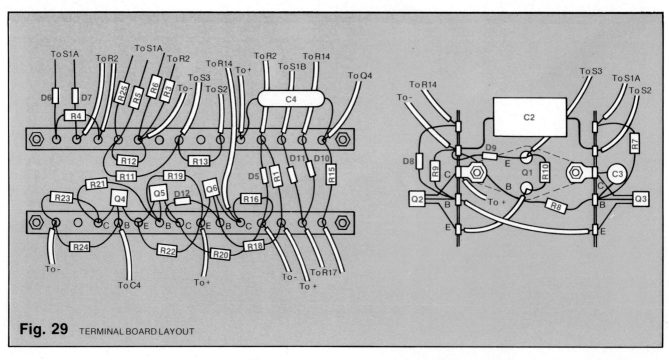

**Fig. 29** TERMINAL BOARD LAYOUT

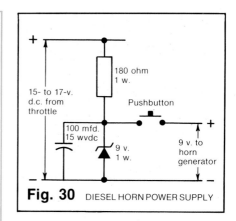

**Fig. 30** DIESEL HORN POWER SUPPLY

(circuit labels: + , 15- to 17-v. d.c. from throttle, 180 ohm 1 w., Pushbutton, 100 mfd. 15 wvdc, 9 v. 1 w., 9 v. to horn generator, + , − )

## PARTS FOR PULSE GENERATOR

| | |
|---|---|
| Q4-Q6 | PNP small-signal silicon transistors, such as 2N3703, BC177 (Canada), or Motorola HEP717. |
| D12 | 4.7-volt, 250-mw. zener diode, such as 1N750A or BZY88/C4V7 (Canada). |
| R15 | 100-ohm, .5-watt carbon resistor. |
| R16 | 6800-ohm, .5-watt carbon resistor. |
| R17 | 2000-ohm, .5-watt carbon potentiometer, such as IRC PQ11-110. |
| R18 | 390-ohm, .5-watt carbon resistor. |
| R19 | 3300-ohm, .5-watt carbon resistor. |
| R20 | 1500-ohm, .5-watt carbon resistor. |
| R21 | 1000-ohm, .5-watt carbon resistor. |
| R22 | 390-ohm, .5-watt carbon resistor. |
| R23 | 3300-ohm, .5-watt carbon resistor. |
| R24 | 33,000-ohm, .5-watt carbon resistor. |
| C4 | 4.7-mfd., ±20 per cent, 100-wvdc, tantalum, paper, or polyester capacitor, such as Sprague 150D. |
| | You will also need a piece of 1/8 " aluminum for a heat sink, a TO-3 insulating kit, tie strips, terminal strips, knobs, line cord, and other miscellaneous hardware items. |

should accidentally be connected to the track.

**Throttle circuit:** Power transistor Q1 (fig. 26) is controlled through Q2 and Q3 the same way as in the previous section. With this throttle, in addition to the d.c. control voltage applied to the base of Q3, there also is an injection point for the pulse generator via D8 to the base of Q2.

The top end of speed control R2 is fed from a fixed 15-volt positive connection. D5 is a zener diode, fixing this voltage regardless of fluctuations in the line voltage. This in turn ensures that the output voltage of the throttle never can exceed about 13 volts even with no load on the output or high a.c line voltage.

Diode D6 provides a much faster action for opening the speed control than for closing it. Resistor R3 provides for a small fixed output voltage at starting, re-ducing the lost space in the throttle control before the locomotive starts to move. Diode D7 bypasses the momentum resistor, R4, for the lost space voltage only, so that this starting voltage always is present without delay, whether or not the momentum is in use.

Brake switch S1 is a 2-pole 5-position switch. One pole is used for the brake function, and the other switches off the pulse completely in the emergency and quick service positions. This eliminates any possibility of the pulses tending to override the positive braking required in these situations.

Capacitor C2 is the momentum storage capacitor; with R4 it delays the rate

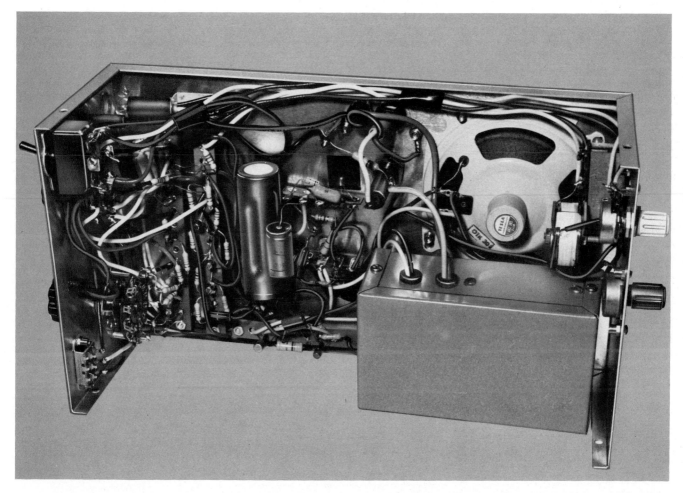

Fig. 31. Although the full-feature throttle, also shown on the cover, looks complex, most of its components are grouped in subassemblies on tag strips. Prominent in this view are the speaker for the diesel horn and the metal box that encloses the transformer.

Fig. 32. On the back are the main transistor and the speaker openings.

Fig. 33. The bottom of the full-feature throttle has knobs for adjusting the pulse width and the pitch of the horn, a button to reset the circuit breaker, and the output terminals.

of change of speed. The momentum effect is switched on and off by S2. When the momentum is off, C2 is kept charged, but ineffective, by returning its positive connection to the output through R13. On many throttles the switching in of momentum while running results in a sudden decrease in speed until the momentum capacitor charges up. With this circuit there is no sudden change of speed because the capacitor is always charged to the correct potential.

Potentiometers R14 and R2 are on a common shaft. R2 controls the d.c. output, and hence the speed, and R14 controls the pulse amplitude. The two potentiometers are wired so that minimum d.c. corresponds to maximum pulse and vice versa.

Diode D9 is protection for Q1 if pulses or incorrect polarity should accidentally be applied to the throttle. Lamp L1 is used as a voltage output indicator, and a choke is included at the output to block high-frequency currents. Therefore this throttle can be used with either of the high-frequency lighting generators described later in this book.

**Pulse generator circuit:** The three-transistor multivibrator generates 40-hertz rectangular pulses. The frequency of the pulses is fixed by capacitor C4. Slower pulses can be obtained by increasing its value, but you shouldn't need to deviate much from the 4.7-mfd. value specified.

The width of the pulses is controlled by R17, which provides a wide range of pulse duration. Very narrow pulses are sufficient for the better-quality 5- and 7-pole motors; many 3-pole motors need a broader pulse for smooth low-speed running. With the broader pulse comes more mechanical noise, so R17 provides a compromise between buzz and performance. Adjustment of the pulse width doesn't change the frequency of the pulse; this is an important feature of the circuit used.

Incidentally, you may find that some locomotives creep at minimum throttle when you use the broader pulse width. If this happens, add another 220-ohm resistor across R3, or short-circuit R3 entirely.

**Construction:** Fig. 31 illustrates the general method of assembly. The aluminum cabinet can be mounted either vertically or horizontally. For now, think of the panel with the controls as the top and the panel to which most of the components mount as the back. Although the completed throttle weighs less than 4 pounds, remember to provide for the heavy elbow when you mount it to the benchwork.

The power transformer and the rectifier diodes are assembled in a separate metal cabinet mounted inside the main cabinet. The separate metal enclosure is not essential, but it is an added safety feature.

Fig. 32 shows how the power transistor is mounted through the cabinet using a piece of blackened 1/8" aluminum as a heat sink. Allowing for free air to flow over the heat sink in this design is not particularly important because of the large cabinet area, which contributes to cooling Q1.

Transistors Q2 and Q3 are attached to a pair of 4-terminal tie strips mounted on the insulating bushings for Q1. The mounting strips of these terminals are connected to the collector connection of Q1 and insulated from the cabinet (fig. 29).

Most of the components for the brake and throttle controls are mounted on a 14-terminal conical tie strip. Another 14-terminal conical tie strip holds most of the pulse-generator components. These are shown in figs. 29 and 31. The conical tie strips are not mandatory; you may substitute any other kind, but take care not to use any mounting lugs as wiring anchor points. The only electrical connection to the metal cabinet should be the grounding lead of the line cord.

Fig. 28 shows the brake switch connections and the wiring to the two speed-control potentiometers.

**Testing and operation:** Before you plug the throttle in, check the primary leads of the transformer, fuse F1, and the neon lamp. Make sure the case is grounded.

Next, turn the speed control down, turn the brake to release, plug the unit in, and observe the d.c. indicator lamp L1. The lamp should flicker when the pulse-width control is advanced to maximum. The lamp will probably barely glow at minimum pulse width.

Advancing the throttle brings L1 to a steadily increasing light, and the flicker disappears as the pulse reduces.

Short-circuit the output terminals at maximum output. The overload trip should release in a few seconds, and warning lamp L2 should light, indicating the presence of the short circuit. Remove the short and push in the reset button. The warning light also comes on after a short circuit if a locomotive or a lighted car is in the block in use.

Don't forget to release the brake before trying to start the train, because application of the brake disconnects the speed control from the control transistors.

# ⑤ Switch-machine controls

SWITCH MACHINES are most often the next electrical component added to the model railroad after the power pack. They are not without problems. In addition to their unique ambition to burn themselves out, they are easily put out of commission by any accumulation of dust or surplus zip texturing particles.

Both problems can be overcome by simple electronic circuitry. There are further advantages in that with these circuits spark damage or arcing in the electrical switches that control turnout direction is almost entirely eliminated, thus prolonging the life of the switches. Also, only small power supplies are needed as a power source for operating several switch machines simultaneously. With the traditional power system, 16-volt a.c. is used to operate switch machines. A heavy and expensive separate transformer is needed to operate several machines at the same time.

## Switch machines

All two-coil switch machines available today operate on the same principle: When an electric current passes through a coil of wire, a piece of soft iron placed near the coil and free to move is drawn into the coil. Consequently, if two coils are used, one at each end of the soft iron armature, the armature moves one way or the other depending on which coil is energized. The movement of the armature activates the movable rail section of the turnout.

This simple mechanism is low in cost but inefficient. The coils require a heavy current for just an instant — just long enough for the armature to slam into position. Unfortunately, electrical coils have inductance as well as resistance. Inductance causes a high voltage to appear across the terminals of the coil just as the current is switched off. It is called back e.m.f. (electromotive force), and it is usually high enough to cause small

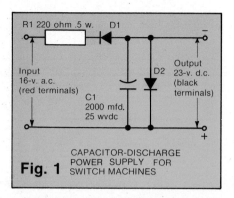

**Fig. 1** CAPACITOR-DISCHARGE POWER SUPPLY FOR SWITCH MACHINES

sparks across the switch contacts just as they are opening. The effect is worse with a.c. than with d.c.

If current is passed through the coil continuously, the coil will overheat and burn out. Some switch machines incorporate limit switches and automatically turn themselves off after the armature has moved. Other types easily can be destroyed if the control switch is left on.

After this story of potential grief we come to the bright side. Simple electronic circuits, similar in concept to those in the battery-operated flash unit used by photographers, enable conventional switch machines to be operated positively, without danger of burning out, and

## PARTS FOR C.D. UNIT.

| | |
|---|---|
| D1, D2 | 1-amp, 200-piv silicon diodes. |
| R1 | 220-ohm, 5-watt wire-wound resistor, such as Ohmite 4600. |
| C1 | 2000-mfd., 25-wvdc electrolytic capacitor, such as Sprague TL1220. |
| Hardware | Four terminals, piece of hardboard, mounting bracket, screws, nuts, solder lugs. |

with minimum wear and tear on the control switches.

The three designs which follow all use the energy stored in a capacitor to operate switch-machine coils. Protective components prevent the capacitor from recharging unless the coil is disconnected or switched off, making accidental burnout impossible.

### Simple capacitor-discharge unit

Take a piece of hardboard 2" x 5", two diodes, a capacitor, and a resistor: Assemble with four terminals (figs. 1, 2, and 3) and install the unit between the 16-volt a.c. terminals of your power pack and turnout controls, then operate as before.

The result? A more positive action by the switch machines, plus satisfactory operation of at least two switch machines simultaneously, even when your 16-volt a.c. power source is the smallest N gauge power pack. Not only that, but the switch machines cannot overheat or burn out, arcing of control switches is largely eliminated, and the train never slows when you operate the turnouts.

**The circuit:** Diode D1 is a rectifier diode that converts the 16-volt a.c. input to about 23-volt d.c. The a.c. input normally is derived from the auxiliary terminals of a power pack, but a separate small 14- to 16-volt transformer can be used. (Don't use a higher voltage, though.) If you use a separate transformer, follow all the safety precautions in Chapter 1.

The 23-volt d.c. charges capacitor C1 through resistor R1, and the capacitor becomes a source of energy.

Resistor R1 limits the current from the a.c. source to less than .1 amp, even when the output of the C.D. unit is short-circuited. Therefore the a.c. source cannot be overloaded or damaged because of a defective control

Fig. 2. What could be easier to construct than this capacitor-discharge switch-machine power supply? On this side are terminals for a.c. input and d.c. output and a mounting bracket.

Fig. 3. On the reverse side of the capacitor-discharge switch-machine power supply are a capacitor, a resistor, two diodes, a short piece of wire, and five soldering lugs.

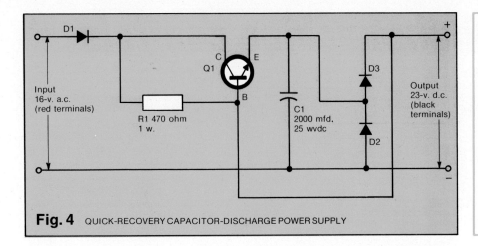

**Fig. 4** QUICK-RECOVERY CAPACITOR-DISCHARGE POWER SUPPLY

Input 16-v. a.c. (red terminals)

R1 470 ohm 1 w.

C1 2000 mfd. 25 wvdc

Output 23-v. d.c. (black terminals)

### PARTS FOR QUICK-RECOVERY C.D. UNIT

| | |
|---|---|
| D1-D3 | 1-amp, 200-piv silicon diodes. |
| R1 | 470-ohm, 1-watt carbon resistor. |
| C1 | 2000-mfd., 25-wvdc electrolytic capacitor. |
| Q1 | NPN silicon transistor rated for 40 volts and 10 amps, such as 2N3055. |
| Hardware | Terminals, hardboard, mounting bracket, screws, nuts, solder lugs. |

switch or a wiring error on the layout. Moreover, the continuous current through any switch-machine coil is limited to .1 amp. Switch-machine coils can stand this low current continuously without even becoming warm. Diode D2 prevents back e.m.f. from damaging C1, by offering a short-circuit path.

Before you switch the C.D. unit on, carefully check that the polarities of the diodes and the capacitor are correct; if they are not, there is a good chance the capacitor will be damaged.

**Connecting to the layout:** Connect the input terminals to the 16-volt a.c. power source and the output terminals to the existing wiring of the switch-machine controls.

Be sure not to reverse the unit end for end; connecting the a.c. to the output end surely will damage it. The two input wires can be interchanged as can the two output wires.

### Quick-recovery C.D. unit

The preceding circuit has one disadvantage. Between uses the capacitor must be recharged through the current-limiting resistor. With the values shown, 330 ohms and 2000 mfd., recovery time is a second or two. In an emergency situation there might not be time for the unit to recharge fully between two successive turnout selections. This variation

of the basic circuit speeds up the charging by a factor of at least 20; the only additions to the circuit are a power transistor and an extra protection diode (figs. 4, 5, and 6).

**The circuit:** Diode D1 rectifies the 16-volt a.c. and produces 23-volt d.c. The charging energy for the capacitor is applied through transistor Q1, between collector and emitter.

Resistor R1 limits the current through a switch-machine coil, should it be accidentally left on, to a low value, about .05 amp. This can't even warm the coil. If the control fails in the shorted position, the transistor cannot conduct and the capacitor will not charge. Diodes D2 and D3 prevent back e.m.f. from damaging the transistor or the capacitor.

**Construction:** The photographs show the straightforward assembly. Take care that all three diodes are connected in the correct polarity. Any reversal here stops the C.D. unit from operating. Observe also the polarity of the electrolytic capacitor.

**Operating:** Connect the C.D. unit between the a.c. terminals of the power pack and the controls for the switch machines. As with the previous unit, you can operate two switch machines simultaneously with this unit.

**Points to watch:** Don't use more than 16 volts for the input. Even going to 18

volts requires a 35- or 50-volt capacitor.

Don't skimp on the wire gauge to the controls and the switch machines. If anything, you need heavier wire than with conventional controls because the C.D. unit supplies a heavier current for a shorter time.

Watch out for Arnold Rapido turnout switches with small lamps built in to indicate direction. The short burst of energy from the C.D. unit will burn the lamps out. Either remove the bulbs or be content to have them burn out.

If you use a separate power transformer for this unit, follow all the precautions in Chapter 1 for equipment connected to the household electrical supply.

### Route control

As soon as the layout has acquired more than a handful of turnouts most of us conceive the idea of route control, as for the throat of a yard, so several turnouts can be controlled with a single button. Route control eliminates a frantic scramble for turnout buttons to push ahead — and usually just ahead — of the outbound way freight.

Switch machines require a heavy current, although only for a short period of time, so if you need to fire several at once you need a big transformer. The transformer must be big not because it

Fig. 5. Except for a transistor, the quick-recovery capacitor-discharge power supply looks the same from the front as the device shown in fig. 2 — the four terminals and the bracket are identical.

Fig. 6. On the back of the quick-recovery unit are a capacitor, three diodes, a resistor, six soldering lugs, and less than a foot of wire. Construction time should be less than an hour.

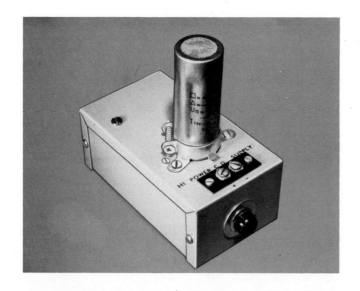

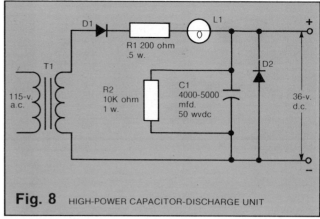

Fig. 8 HIGH-POWER CAPACITOR-DISCHARGE UNIT

Fig. 7. Because the high-capacity C.D. unit operates on 115-volt a.c., safety considerations require an enclosed chassis.

has to supply a lot of power continuously, but simply because its internal resistance must be no more than about half that of all the machines to be controlled in parallel.

Looking at this in figures, most switch machines have a resistance of less than 3 ohms. Six in parallel have a resistance of .5 ohm — 3 divided by 6. If the transformer supplying the a.c. also has a resistance of .5 ohm, then half its voltage is used to overcome its internal resistance. For a 16-volt transformer this leaves only 8 volts to operate the switch machines.

Instead of using one large supply, the cascade method can be used. This requires two make-break contacts on each machine. When you fire the machine for a given track, the contacts on that machine control the next machine down the line and so on, so one button can control a whole route. This method works, but it poses two problems. First, for N gauge there are no turnouts available with the extra contacts required, at least not without modifications. Second, the contacts on many of the machines don't stand up well when handling heavy currents. Heat bends the contacts out of alignment, and dust, vibration, and arcing wear out the contacts. Moreover, you may need the contacts for signals — see Chapter 7.

**The circuit:** The C.D. unit shown in fig. 7 is a higher-energy version of the first capacitor-discharge unit in this chapter. If you use heavy-gauge wire to connect the switch machines, this unit will fire at least five and probably 10 switch machines at once. Because only a small, low-priced 20- to 25-volt transformer is needed, you will not encounter the wicked melting job that can result from stuck contacts with a big transformer.

The circuit is shown in fig. 8. The 25-volt transformer gives 35 volts of d.c. after rectification by diode D1. Resistor R1 limits the short-circuit output current to safe limits. Capacitor C1 is the energy reservoir.

The energy stored in this system is a function of the product of the capacitance and the square of the voltage. The C.D. units earlier in the chapter use 23 volts and a 2000-mfd. capacitor; this one uses 35 volts and a 4000- to 5000-mfd. capacitor and produces about five times the energy.

**Matrix control:** Matrix control first was described by Barry A. Palmer in the April 1965 issue of MODEL RAILROAD-ER. It requires a heavy-duty C.D. unit and several silicon diodes. Fig. 9 shows three possible routes with a pushbutton at the left for each route. The two switch machines have a total of four coils. In at least one of the routes two coils must operate at the same time.

Coil 1R must operate when either coil of switch machine 2 is operated. This produces a paradox. If a direct wire is run from button B to coil 1R and another direct wire is run from button C to coil 1R, feedback results. Push either of those buttons and three coils — 1R, 2N, and 2R — will be energized. Besides drawing a lot of current, coils 2N and 2R defeat each other. You have no control over that turnout.

By inserting diodes D1 and D2 into the leads to coil 1R (fig. 9) you correct matters. Each diode is polarized in the proper direction to let a button feed the 1R coil. Current can no longer sneak from button B to coil 2N as it did with the direct connections to the 1R coil.

This kind of control can be planned for any possible switch-machine arrangement with the matrix method. Draw a grid, as in fig. 10, with a horizontal line for each route-aligning pushbutton and a vertical line for each switch-machine coil. Label the lines as shown. Scanning along line A, put a diagonal black mark opposite each switch-machine coil you want button A to operate. Line A in this case has one such mark at 1N. Line B has two marks, as does line C.

With all the lines in place, look for any vertical line that has more than one connection to it. Put diodes in the diagonals along this line (fig. 11). This diagram basically is another way of drawing fig. 9. The method works for any pattern.

Point the diodes in the direction that passes current from the button to the coil, considering the polarity of the supply. All the diodes point the same way; the anode goes to the power supply positive.

**Wiring:** Many electrical turnout control problems are a direct result of using wire that is too small to connect the switch machines to the power supply. Nearly half the voltage in the connecting wires can be lost, even though their resistance may total less than .5 ohm. Remember to count both wires.

### PARTS FOR HIGH-POWER C.D. UNIT

| | |
|---|---|
| D1, D2 | 1-amp, 200-piv silicon diode. |
| R1 | 200-ohm, 5-watt resistor. |
| L1 | No. 53 lamp (14.4-volt) and holder, such as Dialco 502-9639-0931-102. |
| T1 | 25-volt, .5-amp or 1-amp transformer, such as Chicago-Stancor P6469 or Hammond (Canada) 166G25. |
| C1 | 4000-mfd. or 5000-mfd., 50-wvdc capacitor, such as Mallory CG452U50D1. |
| Cabinet | 2⅛" x 3" x 5¼", such as Bud CU2106A or Hammond (Canada) 1411N. |
| Matrix diodes | 200-piv silicon diodes. Use good quality diodes that can handle a repetitive current of 40 amps, such as Solitron NS2002 or Philips (Canada) PH204. |
| Hardware | Line cord, tag board, terminals, screws, nuts, and mounting clip for C1. |

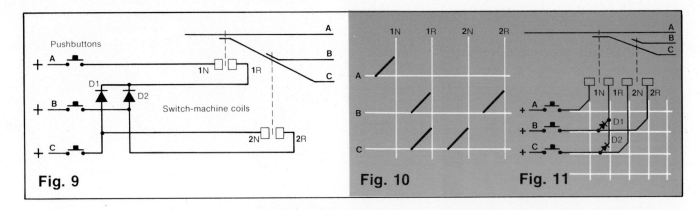

**Fig. 9**

**Fig. 10**

**Fig. 11**

With this high-power C.D. unit, the use of heavy-gauge wire is even more important, because the short burst of current which operates the switch machines is about three times higher than that encountered with a conventional 16-volt supply.

For most room-size layouts use No. 16 or 18 AWG wire, solid or stranded, for connecting not only the switch machines but also the control buttons. If one or two turnouts in a matrix system seem sticky, double up on their connecting wires; that is, use two extra lengths of wire, joined at each end to the original leads to cut the resistance in half.

If you use this C.D. unit to power the matrix type of layout or to operate several switch machines in parallel, you must use a heavy-duty control switch. A standard household light switch works well. You must flick the switch off after the turnouts have operated so the C.D. unit can recharge. Heavy-duty buttons and momentary switches also are available.

**Testing and operating:** After wiring the C.D. unit check carefully that the diode and capacitor polarities are correct. When the unit is plugged in, the charging indicator lamp should light brightly and then gradually dim out over 10-15 seconds. When the lamp is out, the C.D. unit is fully charged and ready for use.

If necessary, the recharge can be speeded up by using a transistor, such as a 2N3055, as shown in the circuit of fig. 4. In most cases, however, the recycling time of this unit should be sufficient.

### An example of a matrix

The easiest way to show how to apply route control is to work through an example. The track plan in fig. 12 represents a main line with several industry spurs, using three turnouts, a double-slip switch (for its elegant appearance), and a crossing.

You can, of course, apply this method to a different track plan, but remember to limit your system to a maximum of five simultaneous turnout throws in any one route. (Heavy wiring and some brands of switch machines allow you to increase the number to 10.)

The six routes in fig. 12 are coded by letters. Route A, for example, turns north at turnout 1, crosses the main

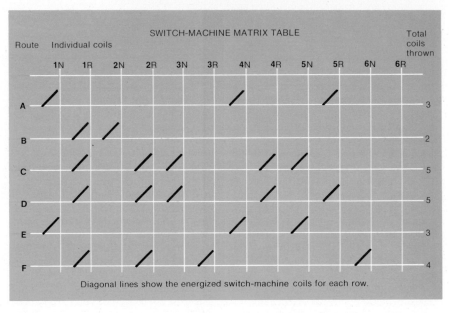

SWITCH-MACHINE MATRIX TABLE

Diagonal lines show the energized switch-machine coils for each row.

through route at the crossing, runs through the double-slip switch, and terminates in an industrial spur. Route D terminates at the same place, but gets there by a different route. You can easily trace the other routes.

Now check the diagram for the codes for the switch-machine coils. For convenience, all coils which direct traffic up in the diagram are labeled N (for normal), and all coils which direct traffic down are called R (for reverse). So, as coded on the diagram, coil 1N is energized for routes A and E, and coil 1R is energized for routes B, C, D, and F. Follow this procedure for the remaining four turnouts and make a matrix, like fig. 11. The scale on the left shows the routes; the scale on the top lists the turnouts and the two coils for each. A diag-

onal mark shows each instance in which a button should operate a coil.

You must insert a diode in every turnout lead that has two or more marks in that column. Thus coils 2N and 3R do not need diodes. The common leads for each switch machine are returned without diodes to the negative side of the C.D. unit. The live leads are connected via the diode to the pushbutton for each route. Routes C and D, for example, each have five leads connected to the pushbutton; each of the five leads has a diode connected in it; anode to the button, cathode to the switch machine.

Fig. 13 shows the wiring layout for the matrix system. Fig. 14 is a photograph of the panel and the buttons.

Worth noting is turnout 6, a switch-back industrial spur. When route F is se-

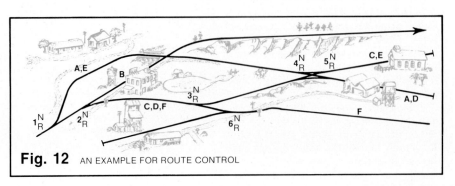

**Fig. 12** AN EXAMPLE FOR ROUTE CONTROL

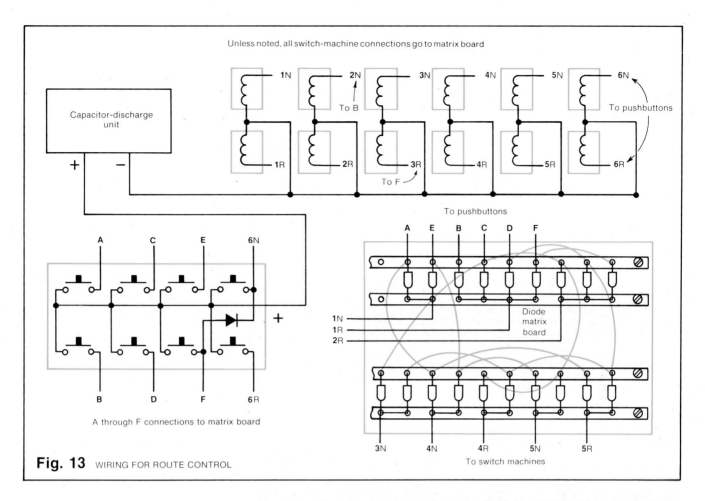

**Fig. 13** WIRING FOR ROUTE CONTROL

lected, turnout 6 obviously should be aligned in the N position, but it should also be operated independently to permit switching while freeing the matrix for other routes. The circuit shows how a single diode couples the N coil of turnout 6 to button F. Two additional buttons can be used at any time to operate the turnout independently.

You can add other turnouts to the system powered by the same C.D. unit. You don't need to wait until the unit is fully recharged to fire just one turnout.

**Problems?** If you have a balky switch machine, position it in one of the routes with a low turnout count, where more power is available to move it. Try not to mix brands of switch machines within the matrix. If one has a lower resistance than the others, it receives the lion's share of the current.

The C.D. unit limits the continuous current that might pass through the switch machine because of defective contacts to a low level. A full 16 volts applied continuously could develop up to 100 watts of heat.

With the C.D. unit you need not wire the switch machines through their automatic shut-off contacts. Another possible maintenance problem thus is eliminated.

Check the double-slip switch to see which coils control which direction; the various makes differ in internal wiring.

If you use Rapido control buttons with built-in lamps, remove the lamps before you use the C.D. unit. Otherwise the surge of energy will burn the lamps out instantly.

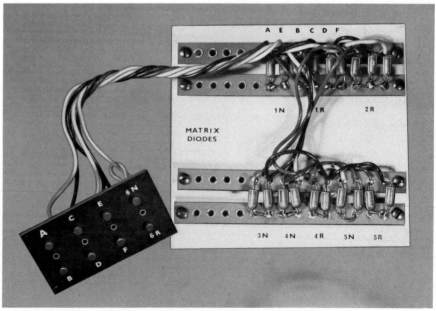

Fig. 14. On devices such as this matrix diode panel, shown with its pushbuttons, labeling with dry-transfer lettering helps you to remember which wires go where. The time and effort that the lettering takes will be repaid the first time you have to trace a wire.

Be sure to use heavy wire. Don't use a common return from the negative side of all the machines, because that would put all the current flow in one lead. Instead, run separate return wires back to the C.D. unit from each switch machine.

# 6 Track detection circuits

TRACK detection is the means of sensing a locomotive or car in a particular section of track so that such items as signals and highway-crossing flashers may operate automatically.

Electrically speaking, as opposed to electronics, only one effective system of track detection is available: A low-resistance electro-magnetic relay switch is connected in series with the running voltage to the track. When a locomotive is in a particular block, its motor current is sufficient to energize the electromagnet, which pulls in its armature and closes or opens electrical contacts. The contacts can be wired to operate switch machines, signal lights, indicator lights on the control panel, and so on.

This electrical system has a big drawback, however: The locomotive power supply must be connected to the block for the relay to operate. As soon as the throttle power is transferred to another block the relay opens just as if the locomotive had moved out of the block. This fault can be overcome with hold and cancel windings, but these rarely are available with the low-resistance windings necessary to avoid voltage drop to the track.

A similar system, with high-resistance relay coils and a separate 25-volt d.c. power supply can be used, but this also detects a transistor throttle connected to the track, so it has only a limited application. It is unsuitable for signals, for example, because all the signals would go red if the power were connected to all the blocks, regardless of the presence or absence of a locomotive.

Electrical track detection, therefore, is less than ideal for model use. Better systems are available.

**Transistor detection system:** One widely used system is Linn Westcott's Twin-T circuit, first described in the June, July, and August 1958 issues of MODEL RAILROADER. The Twin-T uses transistors to sense leakage across the track, with one Twin-T detector per block. The leakage is induced naturally by the presence of a locomotive or a lighted car through the motor or lamp resistance.

Leakage can be induced for all rolling stock by coating the wheels and axles with electrically conductive paint. The Twin-T operates regardless of train direction. It does not detect the presence of the throttle voltage across the rails. If it is sufficient to let locomotives and lighted cars be the detecting elements no modification to rolling stock is required. The end product of the Twin-T is a lamp or a set of relay contacts.

**Light-sensitive system:** Connected to a sensitive amplifier, a cadmium sulfide (CdS) photocell between the rails can detect even quite low ambient light. When the light is interrupted by rolling stock, the relay operates. This system needs no modification to rolling stock and can operate between blocks or even without blocks, unlike the Twin-T. A disadvantage is the problem of hiding the photocells in the ballast while keeping their light-detecting surface clear of dirt. Since both the CdS cell method and the magnetic system described next are completely independent of the actual rail wiring, the rails can be used to transmit sound or light energy in the form of a high-frequency current to the train along with the running power.

**Magnetic switches,** unaffected by dirt and not requiring physical contact with the locomotive, are the basis of a reliable system for detecting the passage of a train. The switches, known as reed or proximity switches, consist of two thin leaves of magnetic material sealed in a glass tube.

When a magnet is brought near, the leaves touch and complete a circuit. The magnet can be mounted under the locomotive or a car, and the switch, which is about 1″ long and ⅛″ in diameter, can be mounted between the rails or outside the rails at the ends of the ties.

In the latter case the system can be made bidirectional, or different functions can be assigned to left and right switches. A complete signal system is described in Chapter 7.

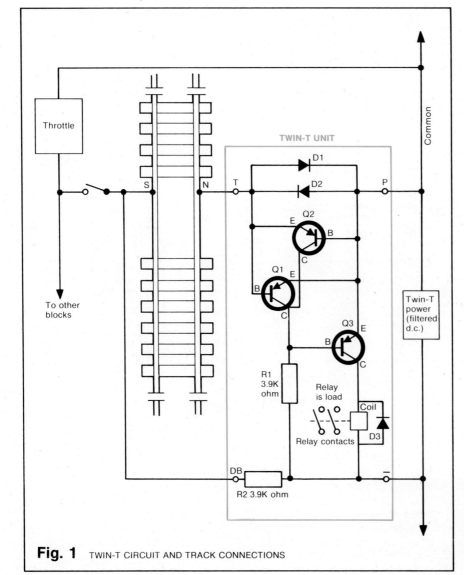

**Fig. 1**   TWIN-T CIRCUIT AND TRACK CONNECTIONS

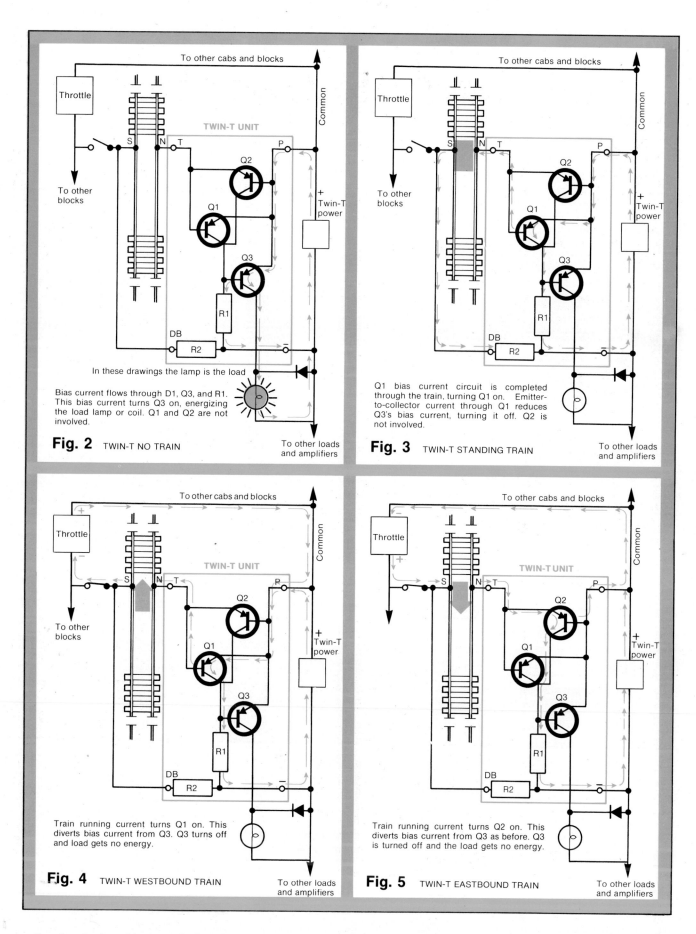

**Fig. 2**  TWIN-T NO TRAIN

In these drawings the lamp is the load

Bias current flows through D1, Q3, and R1. This bias current turns Q3 on, energizing the load lamp or coil. Q1 and Q2 are not involved.

**Fig. 3**  TWIN-T STANDING TRAIN

Q1 bias current circuit is completed through the train, turning Q1 on. Emitter-to-collector current through Q1 reduces Q3's bias current, turning it off. Q2 is not involved.

**Fig. 4**  TWIN-T WESTBOUND TRAIN

Train running current turns Q1 on. This diverts bias current from Q3. Q3 turns off and load gets no energy.

**Fig. 5**  TWIN-T EASTBOUND TRAIN

Train running current turns Q2 on. This diverts bias current from Q3 as before. Q3 is turned off and the load gets no energy.

One drawback to this system is that after you shut down the power, the electronic part of the reed switch system "forgets" so that a "dummy" run is necessary to set the signals in order. The Twin-T system does not have this problem.

**Where to use each system:** Each system has applications for which it is best suited. The Twin-T works best for block-signal operation where there are no auxiliary high-frequency currents applied to the track. The light-sensitive system is best for operation over a train length, as for highway crossing signals or for turnout operation. The magnetic

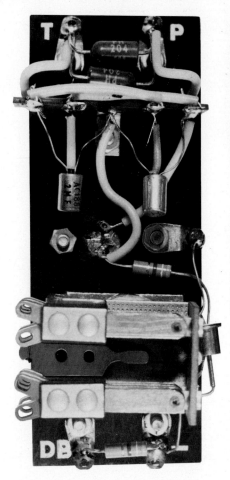

Fig. 6. This Twin-T unit includes a relay. Two transistors are visible on this side of the device; a third transistor is on the reverse side. Its base and emitter pins can be seen just above the relay.

switches are best when there are high-frequency currents in the rails (for lighting or sound) or when a directional system is needed.

All track detection systems are costly, especially if you extend them in quantity throughout your layout. The CdS cell system is more expensive than most, but against the cost weigh the fact that it is the only system that detects all rolling stock without modification. Also, since it has no electrical connection to the track, the rails can be used to carry control voltages or high-frequency currents in addition to the running voltage.

There are other systems of track detection, but one of these three should satisfy any requirement.

This chapter also includes a block-in-use detector which relays a warning to the control panel if a locomotive is in a block, whether power is connected or not, or if power is connected to the block. This is a handy item for layouts with two or more operators.

All four systems require a separate filtered d.c. power supply (Chapter 3). Except for the block-in-use detector, the voltage and current rating of the d.c. power supply is determined by the number of magnetic relays to be used and their resistance.

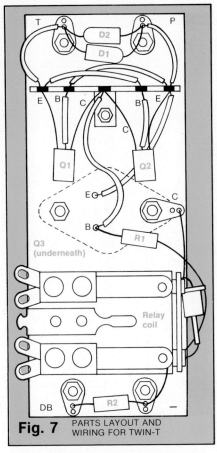

**Fig. 7** PARTS LAYOUT AND WIRING FOR TWIN-T

## Twin-T track detector

The Twin-T track detector unit consists basically of three transistors and three diodes. It is connected in series with the return feeder on the common-rail side of a block. A separate filtered d.c. power supply is needed for its operation; one such supply can power several Twin-T units.

The small current of the Twin-T may be turned off by a locomotive motor, a lighted car, or even electrically conductive paint across plastic wheels and axles. The absence of rolling stock turns it on; it also remains on if power is connected to the block but no rolling stock is present.

The load of the Twin-T can be a signal lamp. Because of its system of operation the lamp should be a green one, extinguished when the block is occupied. The load also can be a relay with several sets of contacts for signal lamps, switch machines, and so on. The relay coil is energized when the block is empty.

**The circuit:** Fig.1 shows the circuit of the Twin-T. In principle it is two transistors, each with its base connected to the other's emitter. Current can pass in either direction across this combination, although only one transistor can conduct for each direction of current flow. The collectors of the transistors are joined. Thus if current flows through connections T and P of the Twin-T, regardless of direction, either Q1 or Q2 will be turned on and current will flow in the collector circuit. If no current passes be-

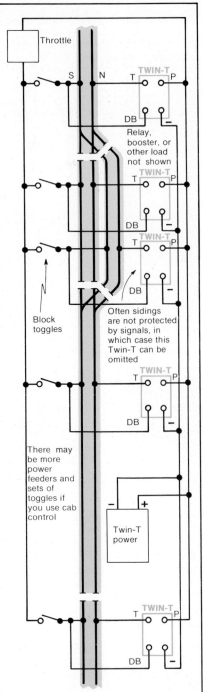

The Twin-T units can be connected between the common return feeder and any part of the N rail regardless of gaps used in the S rail for control. Relays and secondary circuits to them are omitted for clarity. In actual practice groups of Twin-T units should be located in convenient panels rather than strung out along the track.

**Fig. 8** TWIN-T TRACK CONNECTIONS

tween T and P, then no current can flow in the collector circuit. Figs. 2 through 5 show the Twin-T circuit in use.

In a simple circuit the load for the Twin-T could be connected between the paired collectors and the negative power-supply connection. Since the Twin-T is required to detect low currents, however, high-gain transistors would be needed to permit the high current for the load. The Twin-T becomes

PARTS FOR TWIN-T TRACK DETECTOR

| | |
|---|---|
| D1-D3 | 1-amp, 50-piv silicon diodes. |
| R1, R2 | 3900-ohm, .5-watt carbon resistors. |
| Q1, Q2 | PNP germanium transistors with a 25-volt, 300-mw. rating, such as 2N2431, AC128, or RCA 40253. |
| Q3 | PNP germanium power transistor with a gain of at least 50 such as Philips (Canada) AD162 or RCA 2N2869/2N301. |
| Hardware | Tie strips, terminals, hardboard, screws, and nuts. |

much less critical of transistor characteristics for Q1 and Q2 when a third transistor, Q3, is added as an amplifier. It also becomes much more sensitive to objects lying across the rails.

Diode D3 is necessary if the load is a relay coil to protect Q3 from reverse voltage spikes (back e.m.f.) when the relay coil current is turned off. D3 isn't necessary if the load is a lamp or any other noninductive device.

Resistor R2 limits the current that can be drawn from the Twin-T power supply under track short-circuit conditions. Resistor R1 is the load resistor for Q1 and Q2. It can be reduced to 270-ohm, 1-watt if heavy currents are needed from Q3.

Diodes D1 and D2 are silicon power diodes connected back-to-back across the emitter-base junctions of Q1 and Q2. Without them, if a track short circuit were to occur with running power connected, the full short-circuit current would pass between the base and emitter of Q1 or Q2, depending on the polarity of the running power at the time. The diodes bear the brunt of the current, preventing the destruction of Q1 or Q2.

Early versions of the Twin-T omitted D1 and D2. This is satisfactory for N scale and most HO power packs provided power transistors are used for Q1 and Q2, because a small power pack cannot deliver a heavy enough current to destroy a transistor without the circuit breaker in the pack opening. Nearly all conventional 1-amp silicon diodes can stand repetitive peaks of 15 amps or so, but make sure your throttle has a good overload-protection device. In any event, you can use smaller and cheaper transistors for Q1 and Q2 if you use diodes D1 and D2.

The type of transistor used for Q3 depends on the load. In remote instances an unusually high resistance across the rails may not quite turn off Q3. In this condition, with a 12-volt power supply and a 50-ohm relay for the load, Q3 would need to dissipate .72 watt. It also needs to be rated for .25-amp maximum collector current. A medium-power type is therefore necessary for Q3.

**Construction:** Figs. 6 and 7 show the construction and the wiring layout. The relay is incorporated in the layout; it need not be if another location is better on your railroad. Since the relay draws a low current, only thin connecting leads need be used.

Assemble the Twin-T on a small piece of hardboard. Q3 must be capable of dissipating .72 watt at 40°C in free air. All TO-3 case transistors can handle this power without a heat sink.

You may mount all Twin-T units together for accessibility. Remember that connections T and P carry train running power, so for these leads use a wire gauge appropriate to the distance and current involved.

**Supply voltage:** The Twin-T requires its own source of filtered d.c. The same source also supplies the power for the relay or the lamps. For lamps the power supply should not exceed 12 volts; for relays, 25 volts. Any voltage higher than 25 requires increasing the voltage rating of the transistors. A common filtered-d.c. power supply can be used for all Twin-T detectors on a layout. With 100-ohm, 12-volt relays, a 1-amp supply can operate up to eight units.

**Connecting the unit:** Fig. 8 shows how to connect the Twin-T unit to the layout. Twin-T units should be in the common-rail side of the layout to avoid variations in the running voltage affecting the operation.

**Output:** The Twin-T in fig. 1 has a 4p.2t. relay as its load. One pole can be used for a signal lamp (green for energized coil, red for unenergized coil), the second pole for opening the circuit to a short block beyond the signal to prevent an overrun by a following train, the third for turning on the lights at the next station, and the fourth for, let's say, a crossing flasher and bell. With all this activity being automated, the average tired model railroader should have enough energy remaining for a dozen or so switching moves.

**Modification of rolling stock:** The Twin-T operates when a locomotive or a lighted car is in the block. However, protection can be arranged for eventualities such as a switcher leaving a car on the main line or a train breaking in a tunnel.

In the circuit shown, the Twin-T operates with a resistance as high as 150,000 ohms across the rails; in other words, a moistened finger will switch the load. A practical method of making cars conductive is to paint the axle or wheel insulation with silver-based conductive paint. After drying, the paint gives about 5000 ohms resistance between wheels.

Figs. 9, 10, and 11 show methods of painting wheels and axles. Overnight

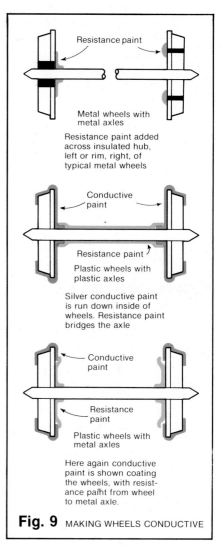

**Fig. 9** MAKING WHEELS CONDUCTIVE

drying is advisable. Test the axle in a Twin-T circuit with a lamp as load. The axle should light the lamp to pass the test. If it doesn't, add another layer of paint.

When this test is passed, leave the assembled car on a piece of test track with full-throttle voltage applied to the rails for a minute or so. Feel the dry paint. It may be warm, but it should not be hot enough to damage the plastic. If it is too hot, scrape some of the conductive paint off the axle.

You may lacquer the axle (but not the wheel tread) for protection. Only one axle on each car needs to be modified; you might consider replacing one axle on each car with a metal-wheeled type, to eliminate the chance of wearing out conductive paint on the plastic wheel.

Conductive paint kits are available from most electronic distributors. The kits contain conductive and resistive paints, lacquer, solvent, brush, and accessories.

**Twin-T tips:** A leaky transistor for Q1 and Q2 may indicate that the block is occupied when no train is present. A leaky Q3 may have the opposite effect. If you build several Twin-T units and want to use low-priced transistors, build one with name-brand transistors that can

Fig. 10. Cadmium-sulfide photocells such as this one, which is less than 3/8" in diameter, can easily fit between the rails of HO gauge track.

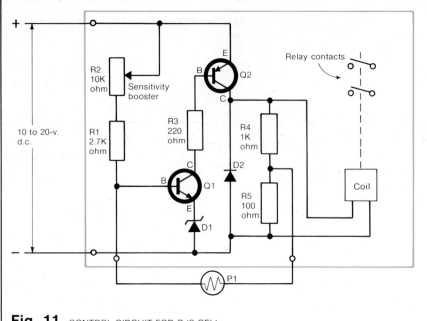

**Fig. 11** CONTROL CIRCUIT FOR CdS CELL

serve as a yardstick to measure the performance of the others.

High humidity can cause false readings with the Twin-T because of its sensitivity. Leakage is likely where two rails of opposite polarity are close, as at switch points and frogs. The unit can be desensitized by increasing R2 to 39,000 ohms.

### Light-sensitive detector

Modern photocells are small enough to fit easily between HO rails, and a bit of electronic circuitry gives you electric eye operation of signals, crossing flashers, and switch machines. Fig. 10 shows the B873107 cell, made by Amperex in the U.S. and Philips in Canada. The two-transistor circuit of fig. 11 works well with almost any cadmium sulfide (CdS) cell.

The CdS cell is, in effect, a resistance, with a value inversely proportional to the amount of light falling on its surface. Typically, the resistance might be 10,000 ohms with a low light level and less than 100 ohms in bright light. The photocell is used in almost all photographic light meters. For model railroad use, the change in resistance can be employed to switch a transistor on and off.

The change in light level that causes the resistance change of the CdS cell can result from a car or engine shielding the CdS cell from the ambient light in the railroad room. The detection circuit operates an electromagnetic relay when the CdS cell is shadowed. A filtered d.c. power supply is required for the unit; one such supply is sufficient for all the detectors on the layout. The voltage and current ratings of the power supply depend on the relays used; 12-volt and 24-volt relays operate on 10 volts and 20 volts, respectively, since relays hold reliably at less than their rated voltages. The circuit has a preset sensitivity control that compensates for light levels as well as for power-supply voltage.

A drawback of this system is that the relay holds only while the CdS cell is shadowed, so that the system depends on train length. The length of operation can be extended by using two CdS cells in series, separated in distance, so that the relay is energized when either cell is shadowed. An example of this applica-tion is found in Chapter 8, where it is used for bidirectional control of a crossing flasher.

**The circuit:** Figs. 11, 12, and 13 show the CdS detection unit. It operates as follows. When the light level is high, the resistance of the cell is low. Under these conditions transistor Q1 (and thus Q2) is held in its nonconducting condition by adjusting the sensitivity control, R2, so that the voltage between the negative supply and the base of Q1 is a volt or so higher than that developed across zener diode D1. The base of Q1 is returned to the negative supply through the CdS cell and R1. When the light level drops, the voltage on the base of Q1 changes because the CdS cell resistance goes up, so Q1 and Q2 begin to conduct. As Q2 starts conducting, the voltage change resulting across R1 is fed to the base of Q1 through the CdS cell. This process produces a snap action, and the relay or light in the load circuit operates immediately. Electronically speaking, the circuit is a Schmitt trigger circuit. Zener

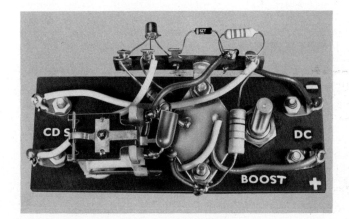

Fig. 12. The CdS detector unit shown here includes a relay, just to the right of the terminals marked CDS.

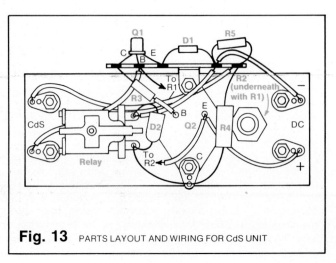

**Fig. 13** PARTS LAYOUT AND WIRING FOR CdS UNIT

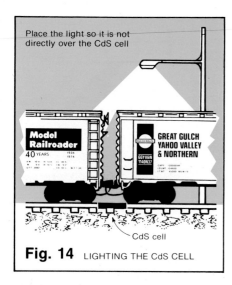

Place the light so it is not directly over the CdS cell

Model Railroader
40 YEARS 1934 1974

GREAT GULCH YAHOO VALLEY & NORTHERN

CdS cell

**Fig. 14** LIGHTING THE CdS CELL

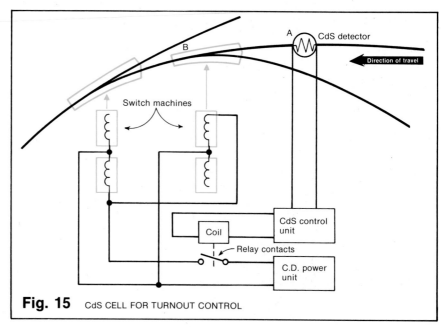

A CdS detector
B
Direction of travel
Switch machines
Coil
CdS control unit
Relay contacts
C.D. power unit

**Fig. 15** CdS CELL FOR TURNOUT CONTROL

diode D1 assists in making the circuit substantially independent of the supply voltage.

**Sensitivity:** This track detector is sensitive enough to stay off with even the low ambient-light conditions of most layouts. For "night" operations an overhead yard light or trackside light is necessary to keep the resistance of the CdS cell low. The sensitivity is impaired if the surface of the cell is covered with ballast, so be careful if you conceal the unit beneath the ties.

To avoid chattering of the relay caused by light filtering through the gaps between moving cars, place the light so it is not directly over the photocell (fig. 14). In addition, some side-shielding with a building or a bit of scenery will help give reliable and consistent operation.

Construction of the unit is a simple process. The wiring diagram, photograph, and parts list should provide all the guidance you need.

**Applications:** The CdS detector is most useful for short-duration operations, such as turning on crossing flashers. It can also be used for automatic turnout selection, provided a separate C.D. power supply is used for the turnouts. A train stopped over the CdS cell would leave the switch machine connected to the power, and the conventional method of supplying 16-volt a.c. would result in a burned-out switch machine.

Fig. 15 shows a suitable application. A westbound train shadows the cell at A, activating the relay and thus the switch machine. Extra contacts on the relay can be used for the signal at B. The green aspect shows after the turnout has thrown; yellow or red shows before and after the train passes over the cell. The C.D. unit recharges after the train has cleared the photocell at A. The turnout also can be thrown conventionally with pushbuttons. The C.D. unit has enough power for two switch machines, so route selection can be extended to the next turnout, too. A high-powered C.D. unit can work

## PARTS FOR LIGHT-SENSITIVE TRACK DETECTOR

| | |
|---|---|
| Q1 | NPN small-signal silicon transistor with a 40-volt, 300-mw. rating, such as Sylvania ECG123 or Philips (Canada) BC107. |
| Q2 | PNP power transistor, such as Sylvania ECG121, Delco DTG-110, or Philips (Canada) AD149. |
| D1 | For 10-volt power supply, use a 6.2-volt, .25-watt zener diode, such as IRC 1N707 or Philips (Canada) BZY88/C6V2. For 20-volt power supply, use a 10-volt, .25-watt zener diode, such as IRC 1N715 or Philips BZY/C10. |
| D2 | 200-piv silicon diode. |
| P1 | Cadmium sulfide cell with a sensitivity of 600 ohms maximum at 50 lux, such as Amperex or Philips B873107 or RPY58A. |
| R1 | 2700-ohm, .5-watt carbon resistor. |
| R2 | 10,000-ohm linear-taper carbon potentiometer. |
| R3 | 220-ohm, .5-watt carbon resistor. |
| R4 | 1000-ohm, 1-watt carbon resistor. |
| R5 | 100-ohm, .5-watt carbon resistor. |
| Hardware | Tie strips, mounting plate, hardboard, relay, and other items. |

several switch machines at once, to give you automatic route selection through a complicated junction.

## Magnetic switch detection

Switch contacts located at the rail and operated by the pressure of wheel flanges have been used for many years. Normally they consist of a phosphor-bronze contact finger that produces electrical continuity when a metal wheel passes between it and the rail edge.

The magnetic reed switch is a sophisticated version of the flange-operated switch. Switch contacts welded to magnetic strip material are sealed inside a small glass tube (fig. 16). When a magnet is brought near the switch, the contacts close. If the switch is located on the ties and a magnet is attached to the bottom of a car or engine, the switch can respond to the passage of the train.

Naturally such a switch, as it stands, has limited use, since it makes contact for only a short time.

However, with the addition of electronics, the switch position can be stored

or remembered until a canceling signal arrives. Once the switch has been triggered, the electronic part of the detector circuit stops in the mode selected by the switch, even though that switch may open and close several more times. Another magnetic switch can be used to cancel the first, changing the setting of the detector.

As with the other two systems described, the end device in the control

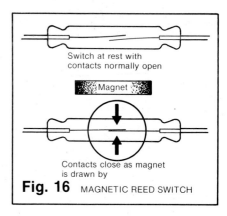

Switch at rest with contacts normally open

Magnet

Contacts close as magnet is drawn by

**Fig. 16** MAGNETIC REED SWITCH

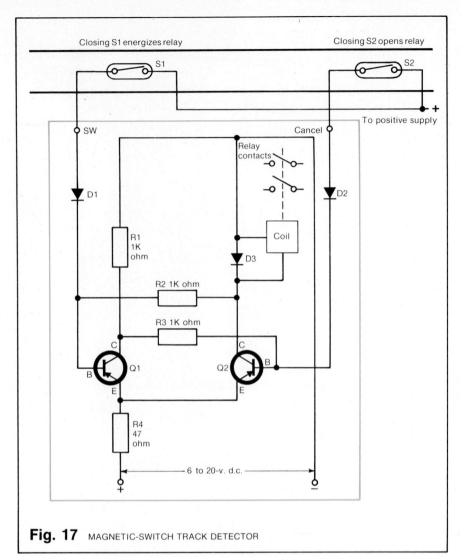

**Fig. 17** MAGNETIC-SWITCH TRACK DETECTOR

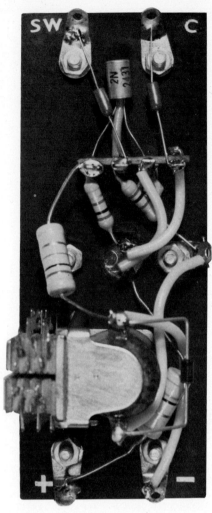

Fig. 18. This detector unit is designed for use with magnetic reed switches.

**PARTS FOR MAGNETIC REED SWITCH TRACK DETECTOR**

| | |
|---|---|
| D1, D2 | Low-leakage silicon diodes rated at least 50-piv. |
| D3 | 100-piv, 1-amp silicon diode. |
| R1 | 1000-ohm, 1-watt carbon resistor. |
| R2, R3 | 1000-ohm, .5-watt carbon resistor. |
| R4 | 47-ohm, 1-watt carbon resistor. |
| Q1 | PNP high-gain germanium transistor with a 25-volt, 300-mw. rating, such as 2N2429 or 2N4106. |
| Q2 | PNP power transistor with a 40-volt rating and a gain of at least 80, such as Sylvania ECG121 or 2N2836. |
| S1, S2 | Magnetic reed switches. |
| Hardware | Tag strips, hardboard, relay, and other items. |

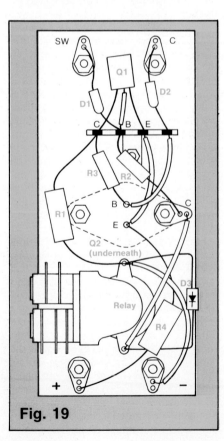

**Fig. 19**

chain is a relay, though this particular circuit also can be used for switching lamps. Chapter 7 describes two signal circuits based on this feature.

This method of detection has another advantage. By offsetting the switches to one side of the track and mounting the magnets in corresponding positions, different functions can be performed in each direction. You also can have automatic route control, although locomotives always must be operated, for example, long hood forward or certain locomotives must be assigned to the main line and others to the branch. In addi-

tion, you can equip a box car or an express reefer with a magnet and couple the car right behind a locomotive that doesn't have a magnet — in case your friends bring locomotives with them when they visit your layout.

The magnetic reed switch system is isolated from the running power, so the rails can carry high-frequency lighting or sound power without interfering with track detection.

It is possible to use the flange-operated switch and still retain the benefit of isolation from the track voltage. Even though one rail is connected to the

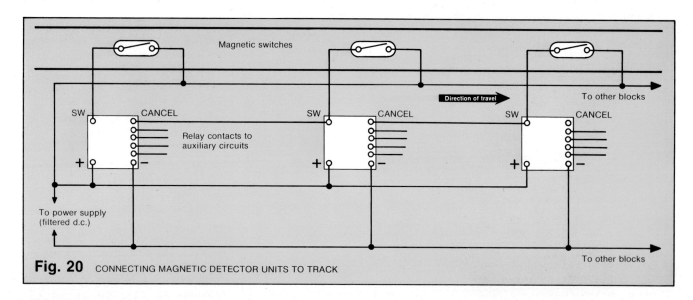

**Fig. 20** CONNECTING MAGNETIC DETECTOR UNITS TO TRACK

detection system, the track voltage does not affect the operation if no other common contact exists between the track and the power supply for the track detection electronics. The electronic unit is sensitive enough to operate even with a dirty rail contact, which is more than can be said for the original electrical-only concept of this simple type of switch.

**The circuit:** The circuit for the track detector unit is shown in fig. 17. Two PNP germanium transistors are used. Q2, which operates the relay, is a power type because it may have to handle high currents. The transistors are connected in what is termed a "flip-flop" circuit. Only one transistor can be turned on at a time, because the collector-to-base interconnections between the two devices operate so that one device is turned off by the voltage on its base when the other's collector voltage falls toward its emitter voltage.

Diode D1 allows the power supply positive to be connected momentarily when a passing magnet closes S1. This positive pulse applied to the base of Q1 turns the transistor off. It stops conducting, so consequently Q2 turns on and the relay coil is energized.

The coil remains energized until the base of Q2 receives a positive pulse on its base from S2. Q2 turns off, the relay coil is de-energized, and Q1 turns on again.

The filtered d.c. power supply for the track detector unit can range from 6 to 20 volts or so; its actual voltage and current rating depend on the relays you use. If you can obtain relay coils with 1000 ohms resistance for 20-volt operation, you can use an ordinary .5-watt transistor for Q2. A 1-amp supply will suffice for 20 units. Diode D3 protects Q2 from back e.m.f. when the relay coil is de-energized.

**Construction:** The assembly is shown in figs. 18 and 19. The unit shown is mounted on a piece of hardboard 2" x 5" — size is not critical. The power

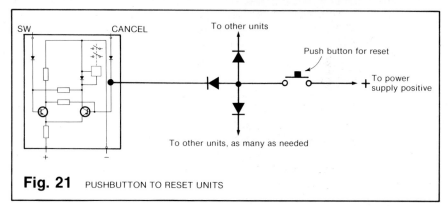

**Fig. 21** PUSHBUTTON TO RESET UNITS

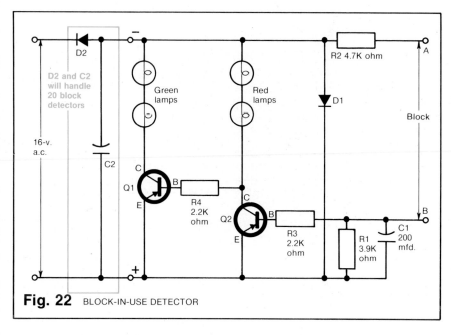

**Fig. 22** BLOCK-IN-USE DETECTOR

transistor, Q2, is mounted under the panel, and its base and emitter pins project through the hardboard. No heat sink is needed.

**Connecting to the layout:** Each magnetic switch can supply a switch signal to one detector and, at the same time, a cancel signal to another, as shown in fig. 20. Thus a train progressing along a track can energize one unit and cancel

the previous one. The action is, of course, independent of block length and the track voltage.

**Electronic forgetfulness:** The drawback to this otherwise simple system is that the electronic units are likely to "forget" when their electric power is turned off. If all the relays are de-energized when power to the system is shut off, then, on the average, half will be en-

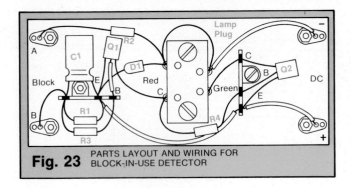

**Fig. 23** PARTS LAYOUT AND WIRING FOR BLOCK-IN-USE DETECTOR

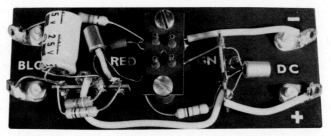

Fig. 24. The block-in-use detector indicates whether anything is bridging the rails of a block electrically.

### PARTS FOR BLOCK-IN-USE DETECTOR

| | |
|---|---|
| D1 | 50-piv silicon diode. |
| D2 | 100-piv, 1-amp silicon diode. |
| C1 | 200-mfd., 25-wvdc electrolytic capacitor. |
| C2 | 500-mfd., 25-wvdc electrolytic capacitor. |
| R1 | 3900-ohm, .5-watt carbon resistor. |
| R2 | 4700-ohm, .5-watt carbon resistor. |
| R3, R4 | 2200-ohm, .5-watt carbon resistors. |
| Q1, Q2 | PNP small-signal germanium or silicon transistors rated .5-watt, such as 2N2431, AC126, or AC128. |

Miscellaneous tag strips, terminals, hardboard, and grain-of-wheat lamps. A 3- or 4-prong plug and socket is handy for wiring the lamps.

ergized when you power-up the system.

You can choose transistor Q1 so that the relay is almost invariably de-energized when power is connected to the system. Alternately, you can send a locomotive around the line at the start of operation to reset all the relays. A third possibility is to add an extra diode to each unit, an extra D1 or D2, with the anodes joined for all units and returned to the supply positive through a pushbutton switch (fig. 21). Pushing the button at the start of operation (or at any time) presets all the units to the energized or de-energized position, depending on which side of the circuit you wire into.

### Block-in-use detector

The block-in-use detector is another easy unit to make. It uses a pair of 500-mw. PNP transistors, a handful of other components, and one circuit protection diode.

Its main application is to warn the operator that a block is either connected to a power pack or occupied by rolling stock. The unit is useful when the blocks involved are out of the operator's line of vision.

For this unit to detect the presence of rolling stock, one pair of wheels of each car must conduct a small amount of electricity across the rails. Any item of lighted equipment automatically satisfies this requirement, as does any locomotive, since the trickle of current for detection passes through the motor, whether it is running or not. The method for applying electrically conductive paint is described earlier in this chapter.

This block-in-use detector does not work if high frequency (for lighting or sound) is applied to the rails.

One unusual feature of the design is its hysteresis effect. The unit always pauses for half a second or so when switching between red and green. This pause eliminates flickering between indications caused by poor wheel contact at the rails.

**The circuit:** The block detector requires a power supply that is completely separate from the power supply for the throttle. If you try to power it from the auxiliary terminals of the throttle power supply, parts of the throttle can be short circuited, resulting in some odd signal indications. The terminals of a spare power pack can operate up to 20 block-detector units simultaneously.

Transistors Q1 and Q2 (fig. 22) are coupled directly so that when one is off, the other is on. Q1 turns on if the resistance across the rails is less than 10,000 ohms. If the resistance is higher — if the block has no power connected and there is no locomotive, lighted car, or doctored piece of rolling stock in the block — Q1 does not turn on but Q2 does, and the green light goes on, indicating a clear block.

Capacitor C1 is used to buffer the switching time to provide a slight delay in switching from one color to the other to reduce flicker. Diode D1 protects transistor Q1 from being damaged by high-voltage pulses present on the rails when using full-pulse power. Diode D2 rectifies the a.c. from the terminals of the spare power pack, and C2 is used as a filter. Note that only one D2 and one C2 are needed for up to 20 block detectors.

Figs. 23 and 24 illustrate the construction of the unit. Use only grain-of-wheat or similar bulbs. These lamps draw about .05 amp each. Higher-powered lamps may overheat and destroy the small transistors specified. One of the first signs of overheating is both red and green lamps turning on together. If your circuit is properly wired and this happens, you may have leaky transistors. Replace the hot transistor, or try interchanging the transistors in the circuit.

As indicated in the schematic, the detector can operate two lamps of each color. The length of the leads is not important. Thin connecting wire can be used throughout, so the second lamp can easily be arranged as a repeater for duplication of the warning on another control panel or as a signal at the entrance to the block.

If you need only one lamp of each color, replace the second lamp with a 220-ohm, 1-watt resistor to avoid over-dissipating the transistors.

**Connecting to the layout:** The two input leads are connected to the running rails on the rail side of the block selector switches. If you use the common-rail system of track wiring, all terminals A or all terminals B (it doesn't matter which) must go to the common-rail side.

# ⑦ Signals for your layout

SIGNALS, whether operating or not, are essential to the complete model railroad — and also to the incomplete one, which seems to be a permanent state for most model railroads. Model signaling is not difficult, nor need it be.

## Prototype signaling

This section gives a brief description of prototype signaling. To explain the subject thoroughly would take a whole book (and does: ALL ABOUT SIGNALS, by John Armstrong; look for it on the Kalmbach shelf at your hobby shop).

Railroads use signals along the line to indicate that a section of track is occupied — block signaling — and at junctions to arbitrate potential right-of-way disputes and indicate the proper speed for a selected route — interlocking signaling, so called because the turnouts and the signals are all interlocked to prevent conflicting routes from being set up.

**Types of signals:** The semaphore signal uses a moving arm for daytime signaling. Near the pivot of the arm is a spectacle plate with roundels of colored glass in front of a lamp for night signaling. Although the color-light signal, which relies on lamps alone, was developed in the early 1900's, many semaphores still are in use — both upper-quadrant and lower-quadrant types.

Several types of color-light signals, with one lamp per color in each signal head, are common. Type D has two or three lamp housings bolted together vertically, Type E has the lamps in a horizontal row, and Type G has three lamps in a triangle in a single housing.

The most modern type of signal is the searchlight type, which has a small lamp, a spectacle plate (much like the inner end of a semaphore blade), and a very efficient lens that projects an intense beam of light down the track toward the oncoming train.

A couple of odd types of signals are worth mentioning. The Pennsylvania developed the position-light signal, which uses rows of three yellow lights that correspond to upper-quadrant semaphore positions. Baltimore & Ohio advanced the idea with the color-position-light signal. It has pairs of colored lights displayed vertically, horizontally, and diagonally, plus supplemental white lights above and below to indicate the appropriate speed through junctions.

Prototype railroads have no hesitation about mixing types of signals. This may occur during gradual replacement of

semaphores or installation of block and interlocking systems. Chicago & North Western uses both Type E color lights (only a few roads do) and semaphores of a unique C&NW design. Illinois Central Gulf's ex-Gulf, Mobile & Ohio line between Chicago and St. Louis was once the B&O-controlled Chicago & Alton; it uses both searchlight signals and color-position-light signals. If you mix types, have a good answer ready for any purist who might come along.

Signals normally are mounted to the right of the track they govern, or above and to the right on a signal bridge. Some roads, though, signal double track for travel in both directions with the signals for the left-hand track to the left, avoiding the expense of signal bridges. Dwarf signals, at ground level, are used only in slow-speed territory.

**Aspects and indications:** Signaling practices vary from road to road. In general for block signals, red indicates that the block immediately ahead is occupied. Yellow means that the next block is clear but the one beyond has a train in it. Green means there are two clear blocks ahead. In heavy-traffic territory many roads use four-indication signaling, with green indicating three clear blocks and yellow-over-green, yellow-over-yellow, or flashing yellow indicating the advance approach aspect. Lunar white sometimes is used in dwarf signals as a restricted speed indication; blue has several special uses.

At junctions, multiple-head signals interlocked with the turnouts show both the occupancy of the track and the status of the turnouts; the latter usually is indicated by displaying the appropriate speed for the route. In general, red, yellow, and green mean the same as they do on a block signal, but the vertical position of the green or yellow lights indicates the speed. For example, red-over-red-over-green means the track is clear but a slow-speed route is set up, and red-over-yellow-over-red means the turnouts are aligned for a medium-speed route but a train is one block ahead. The red aspect of a block signal usually indicates "stop and proceed at restricted speed," while the all-red aspect of an interlocking signal means "stop and stay." A call-on aspect, such as red-over-red-over-yellow, provides a "stop-and-proceed-restricted" indication for an interlocking signal.

Supplemental lights and marker plates on signals give such indications as "take siding," "proceed upgrade at restricted

speed without stopping," and "dragging equipment detected."

Fig. 1 shows how a stretch of three-track main line and a junction might be signaled. Color-light signals are shown; upper-quadrant semaphore aspects are, of course, horizontal for red, diagonal for yellow, and vertical for green.

## Model signaling

In the model world the color-light signal is the most common. Since it has no moving parts, it is the easiest to build and maintain. It is available commercially in most scales. Semaphores and searchlight signals are available in the larger scales, but if you are a Pennsy or B&O fan, you may have to scratchbuild your signals.

The lamps in model signals operate on 12- to 16-volt a.c. or d.c. Simple automatic operation can be arranged using the switching contacts on switch machines. With this method of operation, however, the signal lights indicate only turnout position, which is satisfactory for a junction or a yard but is not much use on the main line. More realistic signaling is possible if, at the ends of blocks, signals can be made to change automatically as trains pass through the blocks.

Simple signaling can be arranged with contact switches operated by wheel pressure, but these straightforward mechanical switches are often intermittent on contact. They require careful cleaning, and depend on either a metal wheel or a locomotive heavy enough to depress the switch. The problems with switch-machine controls discussed in Chapter 5 are magnified here when the switch completes a circuit to a relay, because the pushbutton, operated by a good solid push of the finger, is replaced by a thin piece of phosphor bronze and a locomotive weighing a few ounces. The rail contact switch nevertheless can be used reliably as a trigger for the electronic signal systems in this chapter.

**Electronic signal system:** This chapter describes two electronic signal systems, one for two-aspect signals and the other for three-aspect signals. The two-aspect system protects the occupied block with a red signal to the rear; the three-aspect system provides, in addition to a red signal, a yellow light one block farther back as an advance warning or approach signal to a following train. The three-aspect circuit contains all of the two-aspect circuit, so if you feel diffident about plunging in with three-aspect signals right away, build a two-aspect signal system with three-light signals and wire the yellow lamps in with added circuitry later on.

Both circuits described are one-direction systems, but by duplication of signals and detection circuits they can be made bidirectional.

## Two-aspect signal circuit

The circuit for the two-aspect signal system is similar to that of the magnetic-switch detection circuit described in Chapter 6, with a red lamp substituted for the relay coil and a green lamp substituted for the load resistor on the other side of the circuit. The components you need are:

● Signals with red and green lamps.
● A track detector — either a magnetic reed switch or a wheel-operated mechanical switch.
● A two-transistor, two-diode switching module to control the lamps.
● A filtered d.c. power supply for the lamps and transistors.

You need one of each of the first three items for each block; the power supply — filtered and rectified from the a.c. output of a spare power pack — supplies enough power for 20 blocks or so.

The circuit requires only a momentary spurt of electricity, so the magnetic reed switch and the wheel-operated mechanical switch are the two detection methods best suited for this circuit.

The modules contain only eight components and have five external connections. Fig. 2 shows the complete wiring for three blocks of a main line. The sequence is repeated for the other blocks.

**Track detection:** A wheel-operated switch (either homemade or commercial) can be used as the trip. When the first wheels of the train contact the switch, the red aspect of the signal guarding the block switches on and the green aspect goes out. The electronic module locks in this condition regardless of subsequent openings and closings of the switch as wheels roll over it. The fact that one side of the switch may be connected to the rail does not matter if signal lighting power is supplied from a source other than the throttle pack.

When the train enters the next block a cancel signal is sent back to the first module as the new module changes from green to red.

A wheel-operated switch is not directional, so if a train runs through the blocks in the opposite direction, peculiar things happen. Bidirectional signaling requires duplicate sets of signals, trips, and switching modules, plus a switch to disconnect one set of trips, depending on the direction of the train (fig. 3).

Off-center reed switches in place of wheel-operated trips eliminate the need for a directional cutout. Reed switches cost more initially than wheel-operated trips, but they are more reliable. Either

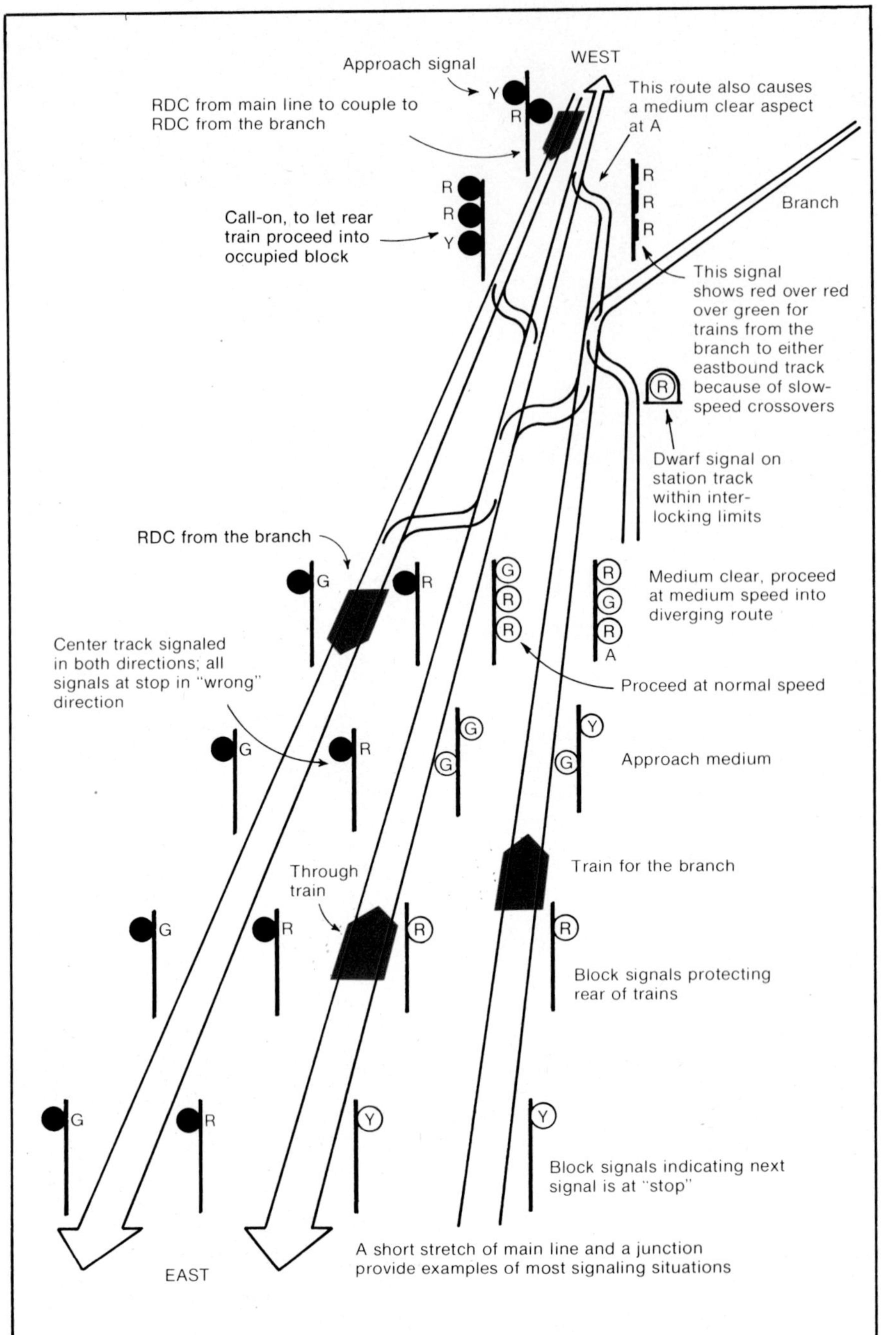

type of trip works with the circuit described.

If you are signaling for one direction only, you can mount the magnets and reed switches on the center line of the locomotives and track, respectively; otherwise, mount them off-center. You may have to recess the reed switches into the ties to clear low gearboxes and coupler pins.

The magnet must be strong enough to operate the reed switch, and it must be high enough not to catch on turnouts and uncoupling ramps. Do not mix types of switches or magnets, since different types of switches require different levels of magnetism to operate. A good type of magnet is the beam bender magnet used for correcting distortion on television tube deflection yokes. Most electronics

supply houses offer this type of magnet.

**The circuit:** The transistors used are general purpose silicon NPN types. A pair is operated as a flip-flop circuit. When one transistor is conducting, the other is turned off — not conducting. The red and green signal lamps are connected in series with the collectors of the two transistors. Referring to fig. 2, if Q1, the "green" transistor, is conducting, the green signal light is on, and Q2, the "red" transistor, is not conducting.

When a locomotive operates the trip, the base of Q1 is connected to the negative supply briefly through diode D1. This contact with the negative supply switches Q1 off and locks Q2 on. No matter how many times the trip is opened and closed now, the signal remains red until the trip in the next block

**Fig. 1**   SIGNALING A THREE TRACK MAIN WITH JUNCTION

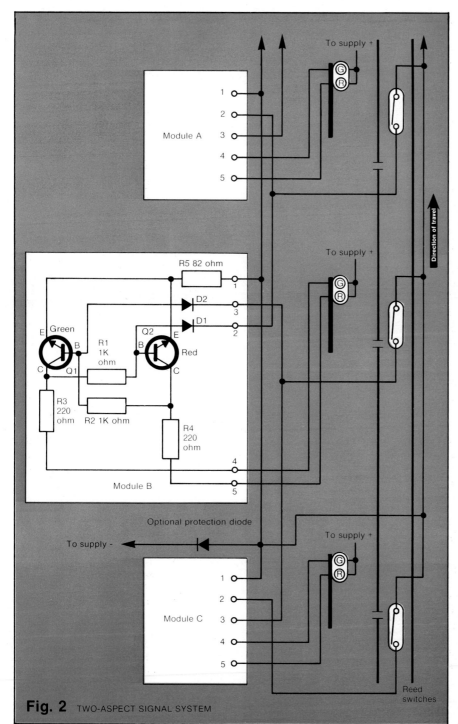

Fig. 2 TWO-ASPECT SIGNAL SYSTEM

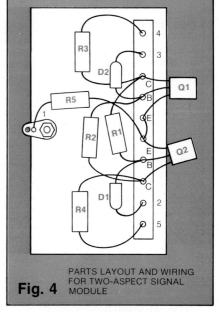

Fig. 3 BIDIRECTIONAL SIGNALING

PARTS LAYOUT AND WIRING FOR TWO-ASPECT SIGNAL MODULE

Fig. 4

Fig. 5. A 10-hole conical tie strip and a soldering lug are sufficient to hold all the components of the two-aspect signal module.

is actuated. That trip connects the base of Q2 to the negative supply through connection 3 of the module and diode D2, switching Q2 off and bringing the green lamp back on.

Diodes D1 and D2 prevent interference from adjacent modules, and R5 provides transistor bias.

Resistors R3 and R4 reduce the voltage to the signal lamps so they burn at a more realistic level and last longer.

**Panel repeater signals:** In series with the red lamp you might consider a second grain-of-wheat lamp for the control panel, to indicate that the block is occupied. Reduce R4 to 47 ohms.

The wiring for this system carries very low current, so you can use thin wire. It's

a good idea to color-code the wires from the transistor module. Consider, too, using five-prong plugs and sockets to connect the modules. If you keep an extra module on hand, you can use it to trace problems by using it to replace a module you suspect is defective.

Construction of the module is simple. Other than the electronic components, all you need is a piece of hardboard 2″ x 5″, a 10-lug terminal strip, spacers, and screws. The circuit diagram and the photograph should provide all the guidance you need.

**The memory problem:** The simple type of electronic circuit used in the modules "forgets" when its power is turned off. For example, if all signals

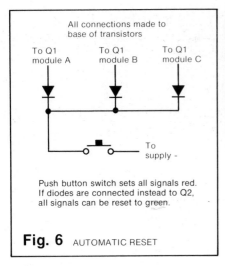

**Fig. 6** AUTOMATIC RESET

All connections made to base of transistors

To Q1 module A    To Q1 module B    To Q1 module C

To supply –

Push button switch sets all signals red. If diodes are connected instead to Q2, all signals can be reset to green.

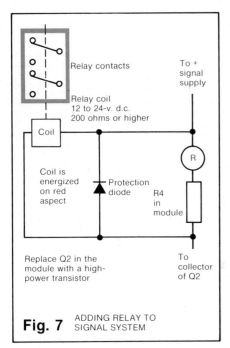

**Fig. 7** ADDING RELAY TO SIGNAL SYSTEM

Relay contacts

To + signal supply

Relay coil 12 to 24-v. d.c. 200 ohms or higher

Coil

Coil is energized on red aspect

Protection diode

R4 in module

R

To collector of Q2

Replace Q2 in the module with a high-power transistor

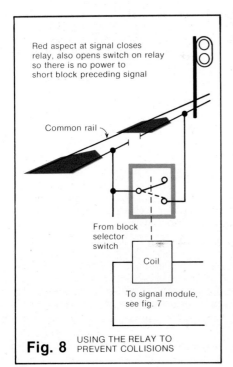

**Fig. 8** USING THE RELAY TO PREVENT COLLISIONS

Red aspect at signal closes relay, also opens switch on relay so there is no power to short block preceding signal

Common rail

From block selector switch

Coil

To signal module, see fig. 7

show green before closing down operations for the night, perhaps half will show red when you start the system up later on.

There are several ways to tackle this problem. You simply can send a train around the main line to reset all the signals. You also can use the pushbutton reset described in Chapter 6 in the section on the magnetic track detection system (fig. 6). A third method entails interchanging the two transistors in the modules of the blocks that change color when the power is shut down.

**Automatic train control:** The same electronic module circuitry can be used to operate a relay along with the signals (fig. 7). The relay should be of fairly high resistance, about 1000 ohms, in order to work safely in the module. The diode connected across the relay coil protects the transistor from damage that results from the inductance of the coil.

You may use a lower-resistance relay, 50 or 100 ohms, if Q2 is replaced by a power transistor in a TO-3 case; no heat sink is necessary.

The relay contacts can be used, for example, to disconnect throttle power from a short block just in front of the entrance to the protected block, to make it impossible for a following train to overrun a red signal (fig. 8).

**Power supply:** You may either rectify and filter the a.c. output of a spare power pack (fig. 9) or build a separate power supply, using a transformer that puts out 15- to 18-volt a.c. (Chapter 3).

Be sure you connect the power supply to the system with the correct polarity; otherwise the transistors will be damaged.

## Three-aspect signal system

The two-aspect system (red for occupied block and green for clear block) is adequate for most model railroad applications. For a long main line, though, it is more realistic to include a yellow approach aspect for the block preceding the occupied one. You may add relays to this signal to arrange for automatic speed restriction in the approach block and also to cut power to a short block preceding the occupied block.

The three-aspect circuit is an elaboration of the preceding circuit. All the solid-state components used in the two-aspect system are used in the three-aspect circuit. So, if at any time your railroad needs to progress to three-

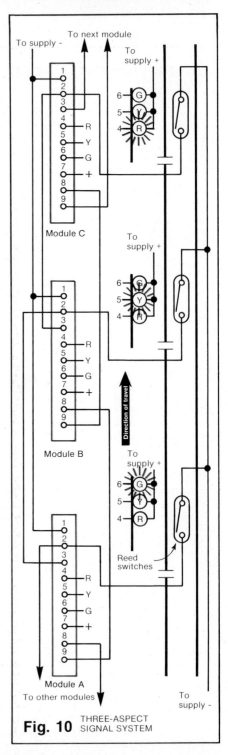

**Fig. 10** THREE-ASPECT SIGNAL SYSTEM

To supply –    To next module    To supply +

Module C

To supply +

Direction of travel

Module B

To supply +

Reed switches

Module A
To other modules

To supply –

aspect signaling, you can use the components you have on hand. With thought, you can even figure out how to wire the extra components for the three-aspect system into the two-aspect system.

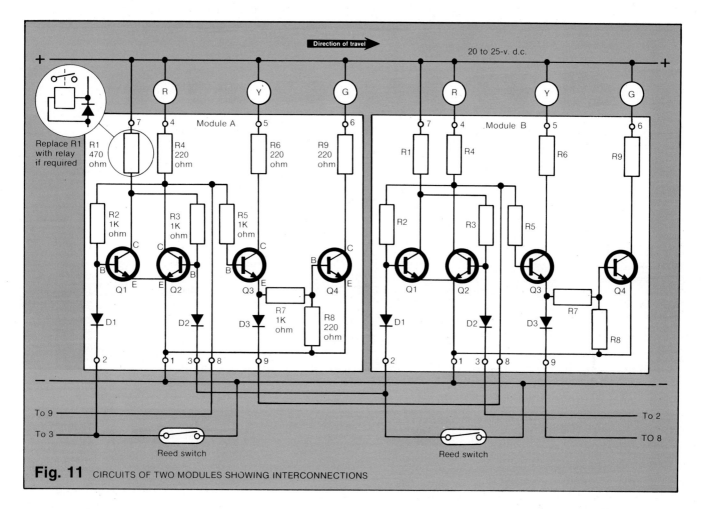

**Fig. 11** CIRCUITS OF TWO MODULES SHOWING INTERCONNECTIONS

As in the two-aspect system, the track detector can be either a magnetic reed switch or a wheel-operated switch. The power supply also is the same — either the rectified and filtered output of a power pack or a separate supply producing 20- to 25-volt d.c.

**The circuit:** Fig. 10 shows the connections of a three-block, three-aspect signal system. Each module has nine connections.

Three connections go to the signal lamps; common return for the three lamps goes to the power supply positive.

Two leads go to the track trips. One trip is in the block the module protects, and the other trip is in the block ahead. The first one sets up the red aspect, and the next cancels it.

Two connections go to the modules ahead and behind and handle the yellow aspect. One connection goes to the power supply negative, and the other goes to the power supply positive through an optional relay.

Nine connections seem like so many more than the five needed for the two-aspect circuit, but each of the four additional wires is necessary: one to the yellow lamp; two to adjacent modules, since they govern the yellow lamp (or are governed by this module); and one to the power supply positive, in place of the green lamp of the two-aspect circuit, since that green lamp is now a block to the rear.

**PARTS FOR TWO-ASPECT SIGNAL SYSTEM**

**For each module:**

| | |
|---|---|
| D1, D2 | General-purpose 40-piv germanium diodes, such as 1N617, 1N618, 1N87, or AA119. |
| R1, R2 | 1000-ohm, .5-watt carbon resistors. |
| R3, R4 | 47-ohm, .5-watt carbon resistors if two lamps are in series; 220-ohm, 1-watt carbon resistors if only one red or green lamp is used. |
| R5 | 82-ohm, .5-watt carbon resistor. |
| Q1, Q2 | NPN silicon transistors rated at 40 volts and 300 mw., such as Fairchild SE4021 or Philips (Canada) BC107. |
| Misc. | Hardboard, tag strips, magnetic reed switches, and a signal with red and green lamps. |

**Power supply:**

| | |
|---|---|
| D3-D6 | 100-piv, 1-amp silicon diodes. |
| C1 | 1000-mfd., 25-wvdc electrolytic capacitor. |

**How it works:** Fig. 11 shows a pair of modules. They are identical; two are shown to illustrate the connections. The operation of the module is complex, but basically Q1, Q2, D1, and D2 act exactly as they do in the two-aspect system.

Refer to fig. 11 and trace a few current paths, starting with all signals green. Transistor Q1 has been conducting because of the positive bias voltage from its base to emitter via the red lamp and R2. This positive voltage is high because the voltage drop across R4 is low. Thus the relay has been energized (or R1 has been passing current) and the red lamp has not been lit. As the train rolls into block A, the magnet on the locomotive

closes trip A, creating an easy path to the negative for the base-to-emitter bias voltage of Q1. Q1 stops conducting, its collector voltage swings up to the positive supply, and the current flowing through R3 puts positive bias voltage on the base-to-emitter path of Q2. Q2 turns on, and current flows through its collector-to-emitter circuit — enough current to light the red lamp.

As the train moves on to block B, trip B closes, creating a direct path from the base of Q2 to the negative supply via D2. Current stops flowing through the base-emitter of Q2, Q2 stops conducting, and the red lamp goes dark. Q1 bias swings up to positive again, through R2 and R4,

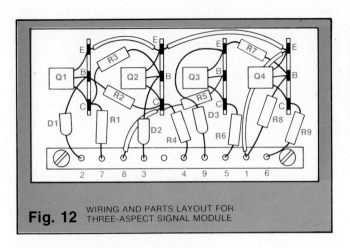

**Fig. 12** WIRING AND PARTS LAYOUT FOR THREE-ASPECT SIGNAL MODULE

Fig. 13. The three-aspect signal module requires four transistors. Constructing the module with one transistor on each of four tagboards makes it easy to wire the module systematically.

thus turning Q1 on and energizing the relay (or passing current through R1).

In block B, the red lamp lights up as Q2 in module B starts conducting. Current through the yellow lamp of block A now finds a path through R6, the collector-emitter of Q3, and D3, and then goes over to module B and through the collector-to-emitter path of Q2 of block B. This current path is open because Q2 of module A is off; thus Q3 can go on because Q3's base-emitter bias is positive, through R5, R4, and the red lamp. Therefore current flows through the yellow lamp of block A, R6, Q3 (collector to emitter), D3, and through Q2 of block B, back to supply negative. If the red lamp of module A had still been lit, the Q3 base-emitter bias would not let it turn on, preventing the appearance of red and yellow aspects simultaneously in a module.

As the train continues, Q2 of block B turns off. Current no longer can flow through the yellow lamp of block A and

through Q3 and D3. The yellow lamp of block A goes out, even though the base of Q3 is returned to positive via R5 and R4, because Q1 of module A is not conducting. Therefore, Q3 still is turned on, but its collector current no longer can flow through the collector of Q2 in block B. It does, however, find a way out through R7 and the base-emitter path of Q4, although at a lower value — not enough to light the yellow lamp. Q4 turns on and allows current to pass through the green lamp of block A, then remains on because of a trickle of current from collector-to-emitter in Q3. R8 ensures that Q4 turns off in the absence of positive bias voltage developed across R8 by Q3 collector current. When Q3 is not conducting or when R7 and R8 are shorted by D3 and Q2 of module B, R8 returns the base of Q4 to the negative supply, extinguishing the green.

**Constructing the modules:** The modules can be assembled quite easily with terminal strips or tagboards mount-

ed on pieces of hardboard. Figs. 12 and 13 show one suggested layout. The layout is not critical, and the lead lengths are not important.

Printed wiring boards may be advantageous for club layouts. The copper foil side of a board is shown in fig. 14, and the component assembly side in fig. 15. The finished module is shown in fig. 16.

**Connecting the circuit:** Fig. 10 shows the connections for the modules, the signals, and the track detector. Only thin connecting wires need be used. Color coding the nine leads from each module is a good idea. You can use nine-pin plugs and sockets, such as miniature vacuum tube sockets. Be sure to connect the power supply with correct polarity.

Repeater lamps for any or all three aspects can be used on the control panel. Simply wire the control-panel lamp in series with the signal lamp and reduce the collector load resistor — R4, R6, or R9 — from 220-ohm, 1-watt to 47-ohm, .5-watt. It should be sufficient to dupli-

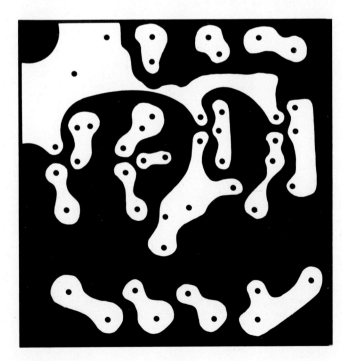

Full size

**Fig. 14** COPPER SIDE OF PC BOARD

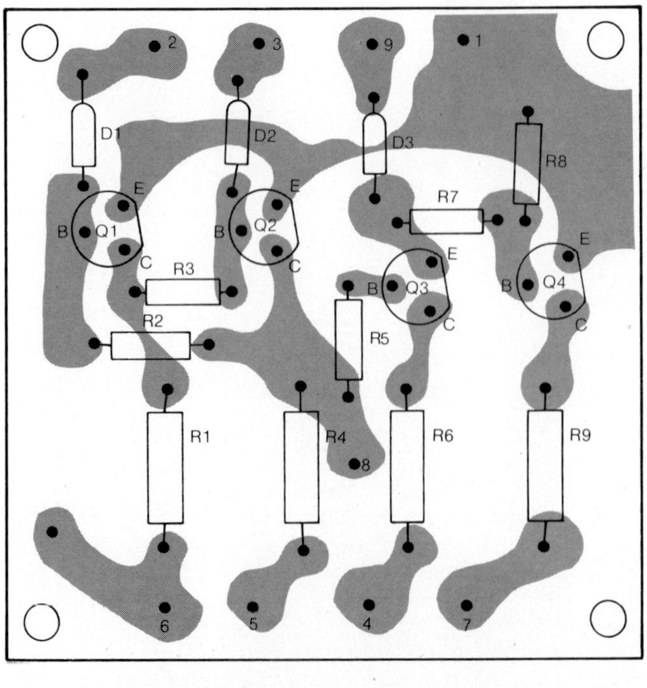

Full size, grey areas are copper on underside

**Fig. 15** COMPONENT SIDE OF PC BOARD

cate only the red lamp and reduce R4.

**Hints:** Malfunctioning may be the result of a burned-out lamp. To test a lamp, place a jumper wire from the supply negative to the collector connection of the transistor for the lamp you are testing. This does not hurt the module.

If you substitute transistor types and use a PC board, note the lead configuration. Not all transistors have the emitter, base, and collector leads in the same positions. If the leads are different, twist them to fit and insulate them carefully.

The three-aspect module is not quite as sensitive as the two-aspect module. However, reliable triggering is obtained with a wheel-operated switch even if the contact resistance is 10 or 20 ohms. The magnetic reed switch is a more reliable trigger, however.

On large layouts there is a possibility of cross-couplings between modules occurring in the power supply. If the system operates erratically, connect a 100-mfd., 25-wvdc electrolytic capacitor across connections 1 and 6, the power supply positive and negative, of every second module.

## Semaphores

Most semaphores are operated by a mechanism similar to a switch machine. They require a heavy current for a short time, and if the power is left on for any length of time, the solenoid may overheat and burn out.

An ideal way to power semaphores is to use the capacitor-discharge switch-machine power supply of Chapter 5. You can use the same supply for both switch machines and semaphores.

If you use either the electronic modules described in this chapter or the magnetic track detector described in Chapter 6 to control a semaphore, connect a relay in place of both the red and green aspects plus two C.D. units. Since the relay contacts stay closed until canceled, the C.D. unit last used could not recharge until the relay changed position.

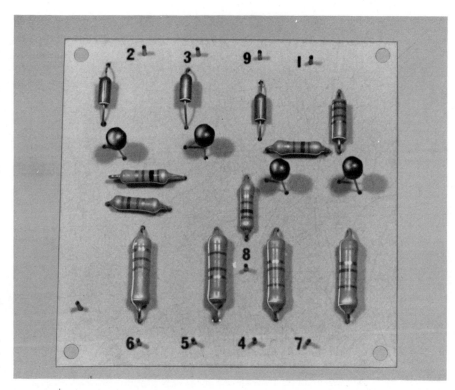

Fig. 16. If you plan to make several three-aspect signal modules, a printed-circuit board makes the construction of the module much simpler.

### PARTS FOR THREE-ASPECT SIGNAL SYSTEM

**For each module:**

| | |
|---|---|
| D1-D3 | Low-leakage germanium or silicon diodes with a 50-piv, 100-ma. rating, such as Sylvania ECG116 or Philips PH404. |
| R1 | 470-ohm, 1-watt carbon resistor. Omit R1 if you use a relay. |
| R2, R3 | 1000-ohm, .5-watt carbon resistor. |
| R4, R6, R9 | 220-ohm, 1-watt carbon resistor if one lamp is used; 47-ohm, .5-watt carbon resistor if two lamps are used in series. |
| R5, R7 | 1000-ohm, .5-watt carbon resistor. |
| R8 | 220-ohm, .5-watt carbon resistor. |
| Q1-Q4 | NPN silicon transistors with a 40-volt, 300-mw.rating, such as Sylvania ECG123A or Philips (Canada) BC107. |
| Misc. | Hardboard, terminal strips, magnetic reed switches, and a signal with red, yellow, and green lamps. |

**Power Supply:**

| | |
|---|---|
| D3-D6 | 100-piv, 1-amp silicon diodes. |
| C1 | 1000-mfd., 25-wvdc electrolytic capacitor. |

Fig. 1. The flasher unit has four terminals, two for input and two for output. It is always a good idea to label terminals.

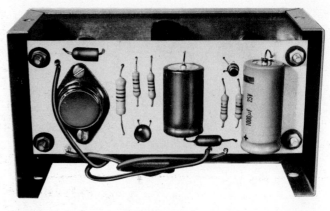

Fig. 2. The PC board is fastened to the top of the cabinet with long bolts, nuts, and spacers. The spacers provide clearance for the hardware on the top of the cabinet.

# (8) *Lighting systems and a diesel horn*

THE circuits in this chapter are designed to add to the visual and auditory effect of the model railroad. The circuits are simple ones; Chapter 9 describes some that are considerably more complex.

## Lamp flasher unit

This unit can flash up to 20 grain-of-wheat lamps at the same time. By choosing components, any of six different flashing rates can be selected, from 30 seconds on and 30 seconds off down to about half a second on and half a second off.

**The circuit:** Transistor Q1 and Q2 (fig. 3) are medium-power NPN silicon transistors connected to act as a multivibrator. The collector of each transistor is coupled to the other's base, and as a result the transistors alternately turn each other on and off. The generated signal is coupled to the input of a power transistor, Q3, which acts as a switch, turning on and off in response to the signal from the multivibrator.

The unit can operate on a d.c. input of 2 to 25 volts, depending on the voltage of the lamps you are using. You will find that the output voltage is about one volt less than the input voltage because of the voltage lost in Q3. The circuit diagram includes diode D1 and capacitor C1, so you can connect the unit directly to the 16-volt a.c. terminals of the power pack. If you use 16-volt a.c. input, the d.c. output is about 22 volts; use two or three 12-volt lamps in series to avoid burning out the lamps. In general, a lamp lasts much longer and provides almost as much light when supplied with somewhat less than its rated voltage.

**Construction:** Fig. 4 is a fullsize printed wiring layout, showing the copper side of the board, in case you use the methods described in Chapter 1 to make a PC board. You also may use tag strips if you prefer. Fig. 5 shows the components attached to the board. Make sure the capacitors and the diodes are inserted with the correct polarity. If you substitute other transistors for Q1 and Q2, check the lead configuration — it may be different from the transistors specified. If you choose the two slowest flashing rates, capacitor C1 will be too large to attach to the board. Mount it to the case of the unit with a clip and connect it to the board with flexible leads.

Fit the board into a small case with screws, spacers, and nuts. Mount the four terminals on the case. Use different types for input and output, and mark them. Don't confuse them.

**Using the flasher:** For signs and billboards, use a flashing rate of about 3 seconds on and 3 seconds off. Use two lamps for each sign to eliminate bright spots and to spread the light better.

You don't normally use a flasher for building lights, but it can create quite a realistic effect if it is used for a few lights in the town and operated on its longest cycle. Connect most of the building lights in the usual way, but here and there wire a few to the flasher to give the effect of lights being turned on and off.

### PARTS FOR LAMP FLASHER

| | |
|---|---|
| Q1 | NPN silicon transistor rated at 40 volts and 500 mw., such as RCA 40315 or Philips (Canada) BC107. |
| Q2 | NPN silicon transistor rated at 40 volts and 1 watt, such as RCA 2N3053 or Philips (Canada) BFY52. |
| Q3 | NPN silicon power transistor rated at 40 volts and 3 amps, such as 2N3055. |
| D1 | 1-amp, 200-piv silicon diode. |
| C1 | 25-wvdc electrolytic capacitor. The microfarad rating of the capacitor depends on the rate of flash desired. |

| Rate of flash | mfd. |
|---|---|
| 2 per minute | 4000. |
| 10 per minute | 1000. |
| 20 per minute | 500. |
| 30 per minute | 250. |
| 60 per minute | 150. |
| 120 per minute | 50. |

| | |
|---|---|
| C2 | 500-mfd., 35-wvdc electrolytic capacitor. |
| R1 | 680-ohm, .5-watt carbon resistor. |
| R2 | 560-ohm, .5-watt carbon resistor. |
| R3 | 2200-ohm, .5-watt carbon resistor. |
| R4 | 47-ohm, 1-watt carbon resistor. |
| R5 | 18-ohm, 1-watt carbon resistor. |
| R6 | 47-ohm, .5-watt carbon resistor. |
| Cabinet | 2⅛" x 3" x 5¼", such as Bud CU2106A or Hammond (Canada) 1411N. |
| Hardware | Tag strips, terminals of two different colors, screws, nuts, optional sp.st. toggle switch. |

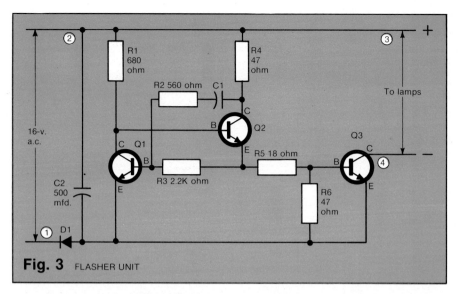

**Fig. 3** FLASHER UNIT

**PARTS FOR HIGHWAY CROSSING FLASHER**

In addition to all the parts listed for the lamp flasher, you need:

| | |
|---|---|
| Q4 | Same as Q2. |
| Q5 | Same as Q3. |
| R7 | 1000-ohm, .5-watt carbon resistor. |
| R8 | 47-ohm, .5-watt carbon resistor. |

**Highway crossing flasher:** The two red lights of the typical highway crossing signal flash alternately about 60 times a minute. For a model you could use two flasher units, one to control the lamps on the left side of the signal and the other for the lamps on the right. However, synchronizing the two units so the lamps will flash alternately is difficult.

There is an easier way. Two transistors and two resistors added to the flasher unit enable it to flash pairs of lamps alternately (fig. 6). Adding the components precludes using a PC board, but since the circuit has few parts, handwiring presents no problems.

### Diesel horn generator

One of the more obvious sound effects for a model railroad is the blare of a diesel horn. Fortunately this is a sound, or rather a blend of sounds, that's fairly easy to obtain electronically.

The horn circuit is really two separate circuits with a common actuating button. One pair of transistors and a loudspeaker supply quite a credible horn sound. But more realistic sound can be obtained by duplicating the circuit, with adjustable pitch in one half of the circuit. The trigger for the horn can be a simple pushbutton mounted near the throttle, or some form of automatic trackside control, such as magnetic reed switches.

**The circuit:** A pair of medium-power

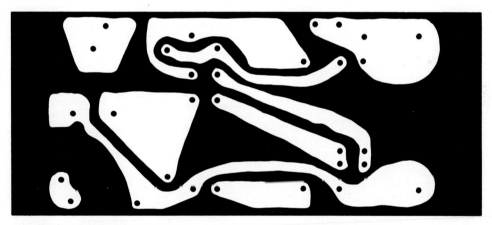

Foil side of board shown, foil areas white

**Fig. 4** PC BOARD FOR FLASHER UNIT

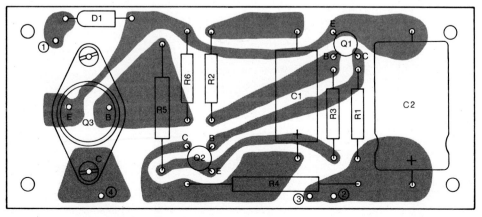

Foil areas on underside shown grey

**Fig. 5** COMPONENT LAYOUT FOR FLASHER UNIT

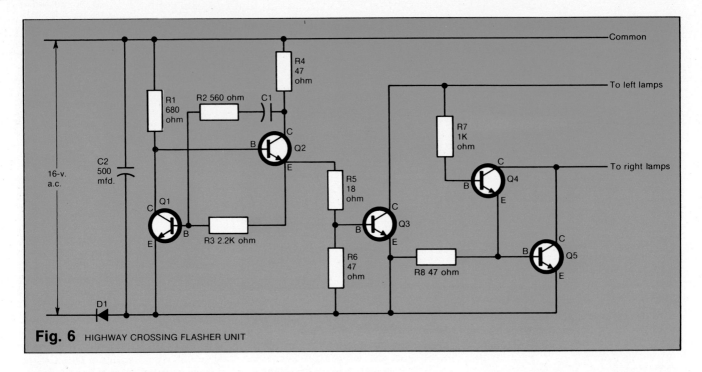

**Fig. 6** HIGHWAY CROSSING FLASHER UNIT

transistors is coupled directly with a small loudspeaker in the output. Output voltage is fed back to the input through a phase-shifting network. As a result the circuit oscillates at low frequency, producing square waves. These square waves are rich in harmonics, so a 300-hertz oscillation also contains amounts of 600-hertz and 900-hertz.

NPN transistor Q1 drives PNP transistor Q2. The types used are not critical. Q1 need be no more than a 100-mw. device, while the PNP output transistor should be rated 500-mw. or more. Germanium and silicon transistors can be mixed or matched in this circuit. Germanium devices give a louder sound than silicon transistors, because of the higher voltage needed to turn on a silicon transistor.

**Construction:** Fig. 8 shows the combined circuit. If the single-note horn is sufficient for your purposes, build just half the circuit.

Two speakers are needed for the complete circuit. There is no simple way of using this type of circuit to feed multiple pitches into a single speaker, because the inductance formed by the voice coil of the loudspeaker is part of the frequency-determining network. Two separate tones fed into one speaker would tend to be pulled together by the common inductance of a single speaker.

If your layout is fairly large, you can distribute three or four pairs of speakers around the track at locations appropriate for a blast of the horn: road crossings, stations, and tunnel exits. A two-pole rotary switch with as many throws as you have pairs of speakers can switch the sound to the appropriate speaker.

**Speakers:** There is little advantage in using a speaker with diameter more than 5″; speakers smaller than 3″ have poor response to the lower frequencies and may lend an artificial quality to the sound.

Mount the speakers on a support board or baffle to aid production of the low notes. If you place the speakers in a box, leave the back open, or the cone movement of one speaker may tend to modulate the other.

Fig. 32 in Chapter 4 shows a diesel-horn speaker mounted in the case of a

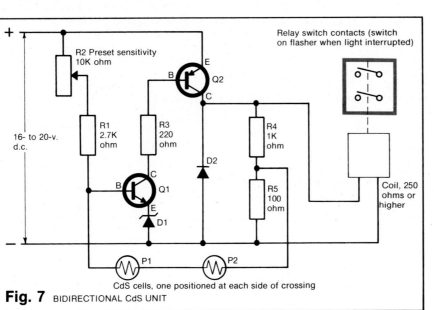

**Fig. 7** BIDIRECTIONAL CdS UNIT

### PARTS FOR DIESEL HORN

| | |
|---|---|
| Q1, Q1A | NPN germanium or silicon transistor with a 20-volt, 250-mw. rating, such as 2N2430 or BC108. |
| Q2, Q2A | PNP germanium or silicon transistor with a 20-volt, 800-mw. rating, such as 2N2431 or AC128. |
| R1 | 100,000-ohm, .5-watt carbon potentiometer, such as Mallory U-39. |
| R2 | 8200-ohm, .5-watt carbon resistor. |
| R3, R3A | 100-ohm, .5-watt carbon resistor. |
| R4 | 27,000-ohm, .5-watt carbon resistor. |
| C1, C1A | 1-mfd., 100-wvdc paper or polyester capacitor. |
| LS | Loudspeaker 3″ to 5″ in diameter with an 8-ohm voice coil. |
| S1 | Sp.st. pushbutton. |
| Hardware | Hardboard, tag strips, battery holder, screws, nuts. |

<table>
<tr><td colspan="2">PARTS FOR AUTOMATIC<br>HORN OPERATION</td></tr>
<tr><td>S1,<br>S2, etc.</td><td>Magnetic reed switches.</td></tr>
<tr><td>Q1</td><td>Dynaquad PNPN on-off device, such as Radio Shack 276-553.</td></tr>
<tr><td>Q2</td><td>PNP germanium power transistor in TO-3 case. The rating is not critical.</td></tr>
<tr><td>R</td><td>100-ohm carbon or wire-wound potentiometer.</td></tr>
<tr><td>S</td><td>Sp.st. switch.</td></tr>
<tr><td>Hardware</td><td>Hardboard, tag strips, screws, nuts.</td></tr>
</table>

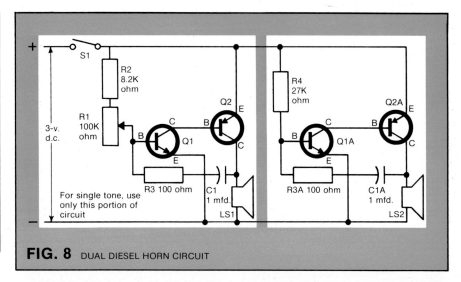

**FIG. 8** DUAL DIESEL HORN CIRCUIT

transistor throttle. Whether you follow this diagram or mount a single speaker near the throttle, mount the speaker so it directs sound back and under the layout. This removes the directionality of the sound and makes it more difficult for visitors to locate the source of the sound.

**Tuning the horn:** Not all speakers sound alike, and possibly you may not obtain the correct pitch even with the wide range of adjustment available from the control. To raise the pitch of the horn, replace the 1-mfd. capacitor with a .68- or .47-mfd. unit. To lower the pitch, add a .22-mfd. capacitor directly

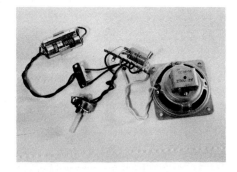

Fig. 9. The parts of the battery-powered horn are shown grouped together for convenience. They can be located as required. A pushbutton may be easier to use than the slide switch which is shown.

across — in parallel with — the existing 1-mfd. unit to make an effective capacity of 1.22-mfd.

**Automatic operation:** The horn generator can be turned on and off automatically by magnetic reed switches located close to the track and operated by magnets mounted on the locomotive (fig. 10).

The following circuit and location suggestions were formulated by Ernest Grande and originally published in the April 1969 MODEL RAILROADER.

The actuating control circuit uses a dynaquad PNPN four-layer solid-state device which utilizes a negative gate current to turn the device on and a positive to turn it off. That's not as bad as it sounds. Reed switches for on or off can

be connected in parallel so that any number of on-off combinations can be used to control the horn, as for example to sound several blasts for a crossing. In addition, you can use one of the switches to start crossing flashers or to lower gates. Chapter 5 discusses reed switches and their placement.

**Horn control circuit:** Fig. 11 shows the automatic switch circuit which can be attached to an existing horn unit. Q1 is a dynaquad PNPN device. Q2 is any PNP-type power transistor. The value for resistor R depends on the characteristics of Q1. The device operates on the same 3-volt battery supply used for the horn. Fig. 12 shows the final assembly; use this photograph as a guide to construction.

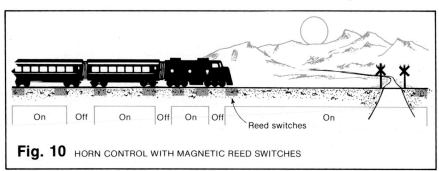

**Fig. 10** HORN CONTROL WITH MAGNETIC REED SWITCHES

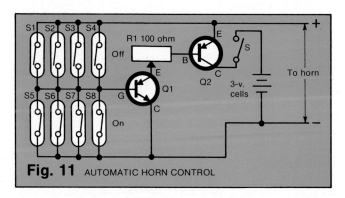

**Fig. 11** AUTOMATIC HORN CONTROL

Fig. 12. The magnetic reed switches shown with this automatic horn switch should be on the track, of course. The dynaquad, which looks just like a transistor, is mounted on the tagboard. The round device is a variable resistor.

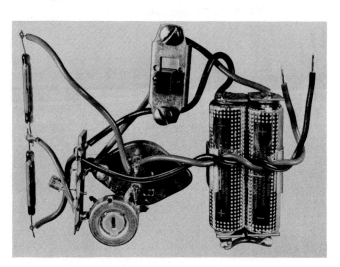

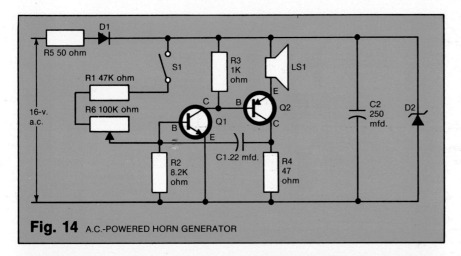

**Fig. 14** A.C.-POWERED HORN GENERATOR

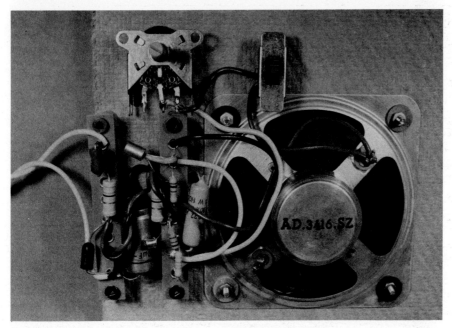

Fig. 15. The speaker of the a.c.-powered horn generator can be located on the layout rather than on the board with the electronic components if desired. Normally a pushbutton would be used instead of a slide switch; automatic switching can be used also.

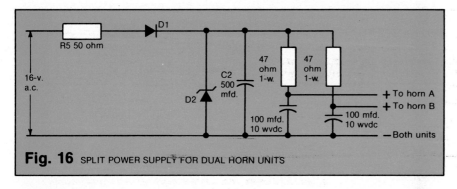

**Fig. 16** SPLIT POWER SUPPLY FOR DUAL HORN UNITS

## Horn generator for 16-volt a.c.

The horn generator just described is used for operation on 1.5- to 3- volt d.c., as from a dry cell or a battery. Many modelers prefer not to use batteries because of the inconvenience of replacing them. This circuit (fig. 14) can be powered by the a.c. terminals of the power pack.

As before, two units can be operated simultaneously to simulate multiple horns, but note that a modification is needed in the power-supply section to avoid electrical coupling between double units (fig. 16). The unit is controlled by a pushbutton; automatic operation is possible as with the previous circuit.

**The circuit:** Transistors Q1 and Q2 are coupled by capacitor C1 so that the output is fed back to the input of the circuit. The feedback causes oscillations similar to the howl of a public-address microphone that isn't shielded from the loudspeakers. In this circuit the frequency of the oscillation is set by capacitor C1 so that the resulting sound in the speaker resembles the horn of a diesel locomotive. Potentiometer R6 is used to adjust the tone.

The pitch of the horn changes according to the supply voltage used. The 16-volt a.c. output of the power pack can vary by several volts depending on what motors or switch machines are operating at the same time. To avoid warbling in the pitch, zener diode D2 stabilizes the supply to the transistors at about 10 volts. D1 and R5 could be replaced by a 9-volt battery, but the pitch of the horn would vary as the battery runs down. Diode D1 rectifies the 16-volt a.c. input, which is reduced and filtered by R5 and C2.

**Construction:** Layout is simple, and the design can be assembled easily on two tag strips, as shown in fig. 15. One tag strip holds the power-supply components, D1, D2, C2, and C5. The other strip holds the rest of the components, except for S1 and R6 which can be mounted at the control panel.

Fit the loudspeaker on a baffle board for the best sound. The impedance of the speaker is not important; 3.2-, 4-, and 8-ohm speakers all can be used. A 4" or 5" speaker is about optimum.

**Operation:** The pushbutton controls the horn. You can, of course, use relay contacts driven by a track detection circuit.

If the sound is too high in pitch, add a .1-mfd., 100-wvdc capacitor in parallel with C1. To raise the pitch, replace C1 with a .15-mfd. capacitor. These adjustments are, of course, necessary only after you have exhausted the range of R6.

### Headlight brightness booster

Lights are a big aid to realism on a layout — in buildings, yards, stations, locomotives, and cars. Locomotive lights, though, are not always satisfactory. During slow-speed yard work they glow only faintly, and when the locomotive is standing still the light is out completely.

This undesirable situation can be remedied in two ways. One method uses the diode voltage-drop principle described in Chapter 3. Although simple, the method does have two faults. First, only those locomotives connected to running power will have lighted headlights. Others that are standing in dead blocks will remain dark. Second, fitting the diodes into some N scale locomotives is nearly impossible.

The other method is to use a small supersonic-frequency (SSF) generator to power locomotive headlights. The principle is not a new one; it was first described by Bob Gilliland and Mel English in the April 1950 issue of MODEL RAILROADER.

**How does it work?** Although ordinary 60-hertz a.c. can pass through our d.c. motors (doing the motors no good in the process), if you make the frequency of the a.c. high enough, the motors will draw no current and will be unaffected by the a.c. However, lamps will light on this high-frequency a.c. Thus, if you send 5 or 6 volts into the rails at a high frequency, the lamps will burn brightly but the motors will not be affected.

**The circuit:** The circuit is similar to the output stage of a medium-power hi-fi amplifier. Normally in an amplifier a portion of the output signal is fed back to the input to cancel out any musical distortion of the signal. If this feedback signal is fed back so that it boosts the input signal, the amplifier oscillates, producing SSF current. With a little judicious fiddling you can arrange the oscillations to occur at a desired frequency.

A frequency of 25-khz. (25,000 cycles per second) works nicely. Any significantly lower frequency requires a large and expensive coupling capacitor between the oscillator and the track. It also reduces the isolation between the throttle pack and the internals of the oscillator. Higher frequencies make the choice of transistor types much more limited.

This unit operates on 16-volt a.c. from a transformer or a separate power pack, or on d.c. from the controlled d.c. terminals of a spare power pack using the speed control to regulate lamp brightness. Do not use the same power pack you use to operate the train. A short circuit of the internal rectifiers may occur.

The brightness booster produces 6 volts on the rails. It can supply about 2 watts of lighting power, which will light five grain-of-wheat lamps with almost no reduction in their brightness, and up to 10 lamps with only a slight reduction in brightness.

Diode D1 (fig. 18) rectifies the 16-volt a.c. input, and capacitor C4 filters the resulting d.c. Diode D1 also prevents d.c. voltage of the wrong polarity from being applied to the circuit if you use d.c. input. If the input polarity is wrong the circuit will not work (just flip the reversing switch and it will).

Diodes D2 and D3 are for protection, should you use the brightness booster in conjunction with a transistor or SCR throttle. These diodes suppress any pulses that might be kicked back into the generator. They aren't as important if an ordinary power pack is used, but they are worth including for safety.

**Wiring the circuit:** Fig. 19 shows a suggested component layout. Most of the parts are laid out on the base plate of the aluminum cabinet.

The two transistors look alike but are opposite polarity types. Don't accidentally interchange them. Secure the two transistors to the underside of the plate which is used to cool them. Since the

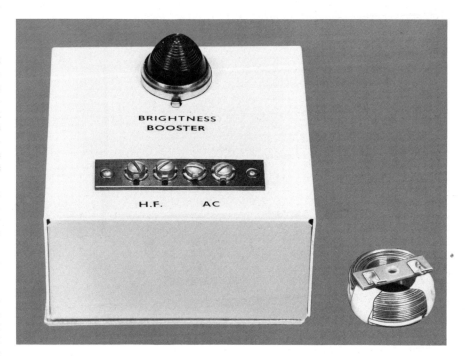

Fig. 17. A choke coil such as the one shown next to the brightness booster must be used to keep high-frequency a.c. from the booster out of the throttle.

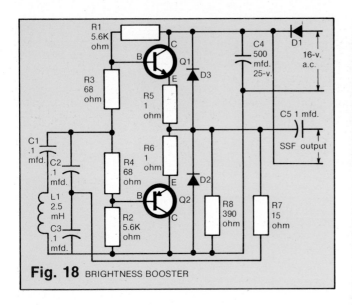

**Fig. 18** BRIGHTNESS BOOSTER

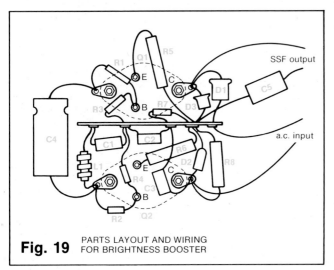

**Fig. 19** PARTS LAYOUT AND WIRING FOR BRIGHTNESS BOOSTER

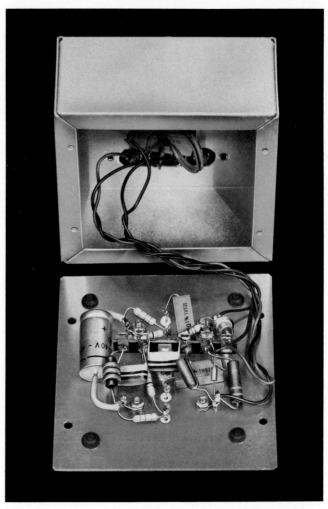

Fig. 20. Most of the components of the brightness booster are attached to a tagboard which is fastened to the bottom plate of the cabinet. Be sure that all the components are insulated so short circuits cannot occur through the base plate.

metal case of the transistors also is one of the three electrical connections, you must insulate the transistor from the plate. TO-3 insulating kits have all the parts you need: mica washers, insulating bushings, screws, and so on.

After you mount the transistors in the positions shown in fig. 19, mount a 6-terminal tie strip on the top of the plate. The positioning of the rest of the components is clear from fig. 19. Be sure to connect the lower items first. Keep all the components about ⅜" away from the edge of the plate so they will not get in the way when the plate is attached to the rest of the cabinet.

Four wires go from the base plate to the terminal strip at the top of the cabinet. Two go to the terminals marked a.c. for the input power, and the other two go to the SSF output terminals, one via C5, which is clamped to the inside of the cabinet (fig. 20).

You may want to connect an indicator lamp across the a.c. input terminals. Use a lamp that does not consume much power, such as type 1819 (28 volts, 40 ma.).

Use rubber bumpers at the corners of the bottom plate to hold the transistor

cases clear of the table. Don't let the transistors touch the layout wiring or trackage.

**Testing:** The brightness booster should light a type 55 lamp (7 volts, .4 amp) or its equivalent quite brightly. If the lamp glows dimly, either the a.c. input voltage is too low or the frequency of oscillation is too low. The frequency can be increased by substituting a smaller choke for L1. If you use too small a choke, though, the circuit may not oscillate, particularly if the transistors are the low-gain type. If you substitute a different choke, be sure it has a ferrite or dust-iron core.

The d.c. voltage measured across C4 should be about 40 per cent higher than the a.c. input voltage. The d.c. voltage from collector to emitter of either transistor should be half the voltage across C4.

**Connecting to the layout:** Fig. 21 shows how the brightness booster is connected to the layout. The output terminals are connected to the blocks through 1-mfd., 100-volt capacitors. These capacitors block the d.c. train power from the booster unit but have no effect on block switching. No capacitors are need-

ed on the common-rail side. In order to prevent the brightness booster signal from getting into the power pack that powers the trains, connect a handmade choke in series with either lead of each power pack. If you have no blocks on your layout, you do not need the capacitors, but you still need a choke for each power pack. See the parts list for the details of the choke.

Rather than try to connect one brightness booster to all the blocks on the layout, you could use two generators; one connected to the main yard lighting a switcher and two or three stored locomotives, and the other connected to a smaller yard and a couple of station blocks. This way several stationary or slow-moving locomotives are lit by one or the other booster unit. On the main line, running voltage usually is high enough to light the headlights properly, but the combination of running voltage and SSF voltage might overdrive the lamps slightly. Do not connect the SSF generator to reversing loops; complex switching is needed to avoid short circuits.

No modification to rolling stock is required with the brightness booster, in

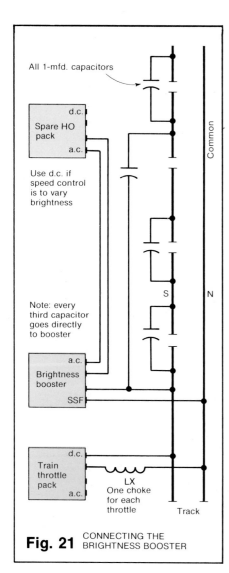

All 1-mfd. capacitors

d.c.
Spare HO pack
a.c.

Use d.c. if speed control is to vary brightness

Note: every third capacitor goes directly to booster

Common

S        N

a.c.
Brightness booster
SSF

d.c.
Train throttle pack
a.c.

LX
One choke for each throttle

Track

**Fig. 21**  CONNECTING THE BRIGHTNESS BOOSTER

Fig. 22. The transistors of the high-powered lighting generator are attached to a heat sink. The ventilated cover encloses the small parts that would be hot to the touch.

contrast to the high-powered lighting generator in the next section. On the other hand, the brightness booster can't provide enough power for a lighted passenger train; if you want to enjoy the sight of a 12-car, fully lighted *Empire Builder* snaking out of the terminal at dusk, you'll need the high-powered unit.

### High-powered lighting generator

A lighted passenger train presents two problems. The obvious one, of course, is that the lights vary with the train speed and go out entirely when the train stops at a station. If your passenger service is anything more than a one-coach remnant of a great steel (or styrene) fleet, you can't use the alibi that the batteries are dead and the car is relying solely on the axle generator. The other problem is that five or six lighted coaches draw as much current as an HO locomotive motor. The amount of power available to run the locomotive is reduced, and a larger power pack may be required.

The high-powered SSF generator is similar to the brightness booster of the preceding section, but its output is about 20 watts, enough to light 40 to 50 grain-of-wheat lamps.

**Rolling stock and layout wiring:** The

SSF energy is coupled between blocks with 1-mfd. capacitors across the insulating gaps. The capacitors block d.c. so that normal block operation is unaffected. Needed in series with each light bulb in the train are small .1-mfd. capacitors; because they are small they can be mounted inside the car. If you have two bulbs in your cars, connect a .22-mfd. capacitor in the common connection for the two lamps. Since the capacitors also block d.c., you have another effect available: You can turn the train lights off and on regardless of whether the train is running or in the yard.

The SSF generator must be switched off for visitors who want to use their rolling stock on your track. If not, their lights will burn with the combined brightness of the SSF and the d.c. running voltage. At low speeds there is no problem, but at full throttle the lamps could run at more than their rated voltage.

**The circuit:** Like the brightness booster, this circuit is similar to the output stage of a 20-watt hi-fi. By feeding back part of the output voltage to the in-

put through phase-shifting components, the "amplifier" bursts into continuous oscillation. This oscillating voltage is the source of the lighting power. With the components shown, the frequency of oscillation is about 30 khz., so far beyond the low-frequency pulses of most power packs that it is possible to feed both supplies on the same rails.

The d.c. motors of the locomotives act as their own choke, so they are not affected by the SSF current. The lamps, on the other hand, operate as well on the high-frequency current as they do on the 12-volt d.c. of a power pack.

Diodes D1 and D2 (fig. 23) are wired across each of the power transistors to suppress any low-frequency pulses that might be kicked back into the generator from a transistor pulse throttle or an SCR throttle. The capacitors used, especially C4 and the block coupling capacitors, must be high quality, either Mylar or polycarbonate dielectric types. Do not use electrolytic capacitors for this circuit.

The power supply for this type of SSF generator must provide 30 volts to pro-

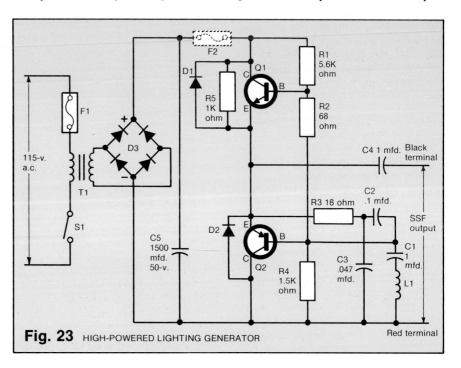

**Fig. 23**  HIGH-POWERED LIGHTING GENERATOR

F2
D1
R5 1K ohm
Q1
C
B
E
R1 5.6K ohm
R2 68 ohm
C4 1 mfd. Black terminal
F1
115-v. a.c.
T1
D3
+
−
S1
C5 1500 mfd. 50-v.
D2
E
B
Q2
C
R4 1.5K ohm
R3 18 ohm
C2 .1 mfd.
C3 .047 mfd.
SSF output
C1 1 mfd.
L1
Red terminal

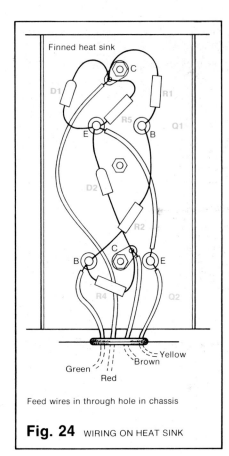

**Fig. 24** WIRING ON HEAT SINK

Finned heat sink

D1 C R1
R5
E B Q1
D2
R2
B C E
R4 Q2

Green — Red — Brown — Yellow

Feed wires in through hole in chassis

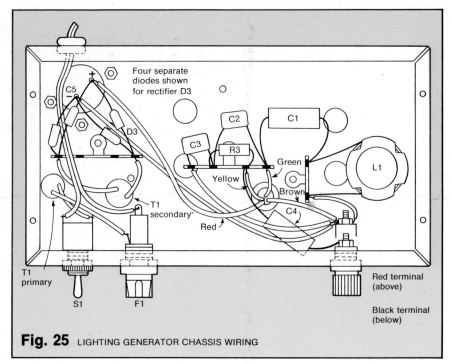

**Fig. 25** LIGHTING GENERATOR CHASSIS WIRING

Four separate diodes shown for rectifier D3

C5 D3 C3 R3 C2 C1 L1

Green
Yellow
Brown
C4
Red

T1 secondary

T1 primary

S1 F1

Red terminal (above)

Black terminal (below)

duce 12 volts of lighting power at the rails. With a full load, 1 amp is needed from this supply. Instead of the transformers specified in the parts list you may use a center-tapped transformer with double the secondary voltage rating; i.e., 50-volt center-tapped or 25-0-25-volt. With the center-tapped transformer you need only two diodes for power-supply rectifiers as in fig. 26. Be sure to follow the precautions detailed in Chapter 1 for power supplies connected to house current.

**Construction:** Mount the two power transistors on a common heat sink (figs. 22 and 24). Insulate the transistor cases from the heat sink with a mica washer and insulating bushings. Smear both sides of the mica washers with a thermally conductive silicone grease. The insulation is necessary because the case of the transistor is its collector connection. Use small angle brackets to secure the heat sink to the top of the chassis.

Be careful not to confuse the NPN silicon transistor, Q1, with the PNP germanium transistor, Q2. The latter needs more cooling, so mount it on the lower side of the heat sink.

Components R1, R2, R4, R5, D1, and D2 are wired across the transistor pins. A solder lug under the mounting screws makes the collector connection. Four color-coded wires lead through a rubber-grommeted hole in the chassis to the other components below.

Mount the fuseholder and the switch on the front of the chassis; both require ½" holes. Drill a number of ¼" holes in

the chassis beneath the heat-sink fins and in the base plate to permit ventilating air to flow through.

Coil L1 will require some adjustment. To start, use a coil similar to LX with about 100 turns of wire. Use an automobile lamp, 12-volt, 32-C.P., connected across the SSF output, and reduce turns on L1 until the lamp reaches maximum brightness. The final value is about 85 turns; the adjustment is not critical. Epoxy the finished coil to the chassis.

**Testing:** Before you plug the unit in, make sure you have followed the safety procedures in Chapter 1. Check the transistor connections to see that collector, base, and emitter are where they should be. Check diodes D1 and D2 for proper polarity.

With no load the power supply should be about 34 volts; full-load supply should be about 28 volts. The voltage

from collector to emitter of each transistor should be about half the power-supply voltage. A big difference between the two means that the unit is not oscillating.

Short-circuit the unit for 2 or 3 minutes before you connect it to the layout. Capacitor C4 should not get excessively hot. The transistors are able to stand harsh treatment, but if you often have short circuits on your layout, add the optional circuit breaker that is shown dotted in fig. 23.

**Connecting to the layout:** Fig. 27 illustrates the layout connections. The block coupling capacitors, CB, transfer the high-frequency current across the rail gaps while blocking the train running power. The block switches function in the usual manner.

With common-rail wiring, the CB capacitors are not needed across the

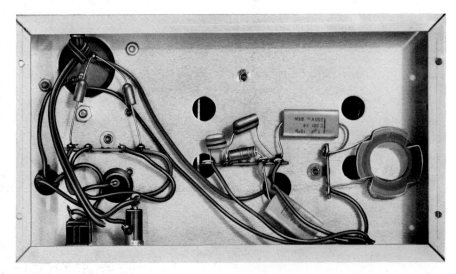

Fig. 26. All of the 115-volt a.c. wiring is inside the chassis. Many of the parts of this particular unit are attached with rivets instead of with machine screws and nuts.

## PARTS FOR HIGH-POWERED LIGHTING GENERATOR

| | |
|---|---|
| Q1 | NPN power transistor, such as 2N3055. |
| Q2 | PNP germanium power transistor, such as 2N442, 2N443, ECG105, Philips ADZ11 or ADZ12, or Elcom ES-10. |
| D1, D2 | 100-piv, 1-amp diodes. |
| D3 | 200-piv, 1-amp diodes (4 required). |
| T1 | Transformer rated at 115 volts primary, 25 volts RMS secondary, and 1 amp, such as Chicago-Stancor P6469 or Hammond 166J25. |
| S1 | Sp.st. toggle switch. |
| F1 | 1-amp, fast-blow panel-mounting fuse and fuseholder, such as Buss HSM. |
| F2 | 2-amp resettable circuit breaker. |
| R1 | 5600-ohm, .5-watt carbon resistor. |
| R2 | 68-ohm, .5-watt carbon resistor. |
| R3 | 18-ohm, 1-watt carbon resistor. |
| R4 | 1500-ohm, 1-watt carbon resistor. |
| R5 | 1000-ohm, 1-watt carbon resistor. |
| C1 | 1-mfd., 100-wvdc polyester capacitor. |
| C2 | .1-mfd., 100-wvdc polyester capacitor. |
| C3 | .047-mfd., 100-wvdc polyester capacitor. |
| C4 | 1-mfd., 250-wvdc polyester capacitor. |
| C5 | 1500-mfd., 50-wvdc electrolytic capacitor, such as Sprague TVL1341. |
| L1 | 250-microhenry choke (described in text). |
| CB | 1-mfd., 100-wvdc paper or polyester capacitors. |
| LX | 500-microhenry isolation choke — one needed for each power pack. Wind 145 turns of No. 16 enameled copper wire on a ⅞″ diameter form (such as a broom handle). Make each layer about 1″ wide. The dimensions and wire size are not critical. |
| Cabinet | Use a ventilated enclosure and chassis, such as Bud CA699, Premier AF-510, or Hammond 1451-14 cover, 1443-14 chassis, and 1434-14 base plate. |
| Heat sink | Delco 7281355, International Rectifier HE-530, or equivalent. |
| Hardware | Tag strips, line cord, terminals, grommets, mounting hardware for the transistor, screws, and nuts. |

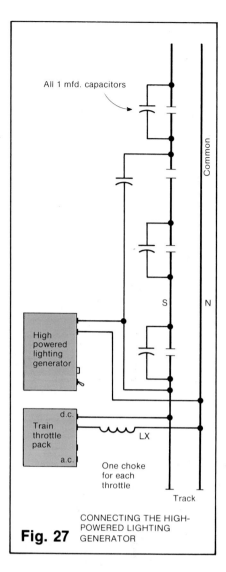

**Fig. 27** CONNECTING THE HIGH-POWERED LIGHTING GENERATOR

gaps on the common-rail side. Omit the capacitors from all four gaps at reversing loops. The lights will go out when the train is in a reversing loop, but complicated switching will be avoided to prevent shorting the SSF in one direction.

Each throttle requires a choke, LX, added to one lead. This blocks the high frequency which could damage the throttle.

All SSF lighting systems defeat directionally sensitive lighting systems, but the sight of a long, fully lighted streamliner should be some compensation.

## SSF and sound

Lighting generators such as those in the preceding sections disrupt sound systems on model railroads when the sound is transmitted through the rails to in-car speakers or when synchronizing pulses are sent back from the locomotive to a trackside amplifier system. "Disrupt" means in some cases "burn out the speaker."

Do not use these lighting generators with a sound system unless the sound system is completely contained in the lo-

comotive and does not connect in any way to both rails. If you use a wiper contact on one wheel for exhaust sound, no problem should exist, but take care that the amplifier and the speaker connections are fully insulated — except for the wiper — from all metal parts of the locomotive.

# ⑨ Sound systems and simultaneous control

THIS CHAPTER describes circuitry that is quite sophisticated. In this respect it differs from the rest of this book. However, developing realistic sound from model locomotives is well worth the investment in time and equipment.

There are several things to remember about sound systems for locomotives. First, for almost all systems, the locomotive must incorporate some part of the electronics. Second, space is likely to be a problem except in O scale. Third, sound signals through the rails are incompatible with high-frequency lighting systems, and the throttles will need chokes as they do for high-frequency lighting.

There are ways around these difficulties. Making a battery-powered sound system is possible, although not in N scale. You can place the components for the sound system in a hi-cube box car or an express reefer coupled right behind the engine. There's likely to be more space in the car than in a tender, and you can get away with wiring perhaps two cars for sound instead of all your locomotives.

## A simple sound system

The simplest sound system entails the placement of several small (4" or 5") speakers at strategic positions on the layout. The sound can be switched to follow a train around the layout.

Your sound can be recorded — either live or from the many recordings available — onto an ordinary low-price cassette tape recorder.

The advantages of the cassette recorder are its low price and self-contained recording facilities. Also the cassette can be changed in a matter of seconds, from steam to diesel, for example. No modification is needed to either rolling stock or the existing wiring of the layout.

On the other hand, the sound lacks synchronization with the activities on the layout. One of the best ways to use this system is to record half an hour or so of activity at a yard or terminal — switchers going past, cars coupling, and the assorted thumps and bumps that bring dismay to the Claims Department — and then play back the sound quietly near the yard on your layout.

Despite its drawbacks, this is the only sound system currently feasible for N scale.

**Wiring:** The add-on speakers should have an impedance rating no lower than the original speaker in the recorder. If in doubt, use 8-ohm speakers. The cone diameter can be greater than the original speaker, giving better tone.

You may include the internal speaker as part of the layout system or you may disconnect it. You must add a 47-ohm, 1-watt resistor across the original output leads to the speaker (fig. 1) to prevent damaging the output transistors in the cassette playback circuit.

Fig. 1. An external speaker used with a cassette recorder requires a 47-ohm, 1-watt resistor across the leads of the speaker. A tag strip can hold the resistor.

Fig. 2. A particularly good location for a speaker is adjacent to a tunnel portal.

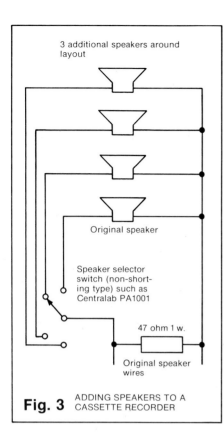

**Fig. 3** ADDING SPEAKERS TO A CASSETTE RECORDER

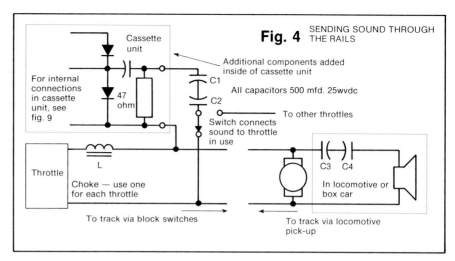

**Fig. 4** SENDING SOUND THROUGH THE RAILS

You are best off choosing a recorder that can be operated either from a battery or from house current. These are safe to delve into, and they are not extravagantly expensive. Using higher-priced, higher-fidelity equipment offers no real advantage in this application.

**Speaker location:** All low-priced speakers put out sound directionally. Directional sound can be an advantage in a few cases, such as the mouth of a tunnel (figs. 2, 3). If the sound is switched to that speaker as the train emerges, the effect is quite startling. In most cases, though, the speaker is better located among folds in the scenery where sound reflection can be relied on to mask the direction. Since the speaker usually will be mounted cone up and magnet down,

like the rear-deck speaker of a car, stretch a piece of cloth dyed to blend with the scenery across the cone to keep bits of loose scenery material out of the speaker.

## Sending sound through the rails

Sound signals from a low-power phonograph or cassette tape recorder can be transmitted to a locomotive-mounted speaker along with the current for the d.c. motor. In essence this system is the same as the preceding one, except that the speaker has wheels.

As you'd expect, there are complications. The sound signal is a complex form of a.c. and could be shorted out through the throttle. A choke must be used to pass the d.c. from the throttle while blocking the sound current. At the other end, capacitors must be used to keep the d.c. from burning out the speaker. The speaker must be small enough to fit into a locomotive, tender, or car.

Fig. 4 shows the components needed. The cassette recorder is recommended so you can tape a program from records. With a little skill you can set up a tape to fit your layout's operation.

Since high power can burn out the

voice coil of a small speaker, limit the power output of the amplifier to 2 watts (RMS rating) or 6 watts (EIA peak-to-peak rating). Virtually all low-priced cassette recorders fall into this category.

**Components:** Choke L in fig. 4 is an iron-cored component that prevents the audio signal from being shorted out in the throttle. C1 and C2 are 500-mfd., 25-wvdc electrolytic capacitors connected in series with reversed polarity, constituting effectively a bipolar 250-mfd. capacitor. If you can find bipolar electrolytic capacitors to replace the C1-C2 and C3-C4 pairs, you will save some space.

Capacitors C3 and C4 are wired in series with the speaker in the train. Fig. 5 shows a 1⅝"-cone speaker mounted in line with the open door of an Athearn HO hi-cube box car. The capacitors are cemented to the inside of the roof of the car (fig. 6). The hi-cube box car permits the use of the largest speaker possible. By running the box car at the head of the train, you can have sound follow your locomotives around the layout. The speaker and capacitors must be connected to the rails, either through a miniature connector to the locomotive or through metal wheels and axles of the

Fig. 5. An HO scale hi-cube box car can contain a small speaker.

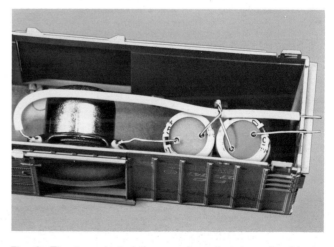

Fig. 6. The two electrolytic capacitors that form the bipolar capacitor which blocks the running voltage can be cemented to the inside of the roof of the hi-cube box car.

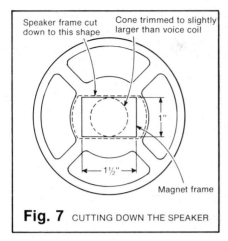

**Fig. 7** CUTTING DOWN THE SPEAKER

box car. The speaker gives the car enough weight to pick up current reliably.

The choke, L, must be low resistance, no more than 2 ohms, to avoid voltage drop at full throttle current. A replacement output transformer from a transistor car radio is ideal. Most have three connections, with one connection a pair of leads. Use the two single-lead connections. Chicago-Stancor TA-50 and Hammond (Canada) 147-J are suitable; use only the primary leads on the Hammond component.

**The speaker** is a moving-coil type headphone insert. The one shown is a Sharpe. These are easily obtainable, and they have a wide frequency range. Some small speakers are specially designed for use as tweeters and have little low-frequency output.

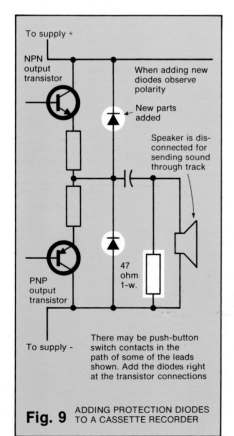

**Fig. 9** ADDING PROTECTION DIODES TO A CASSETTE RECORDER

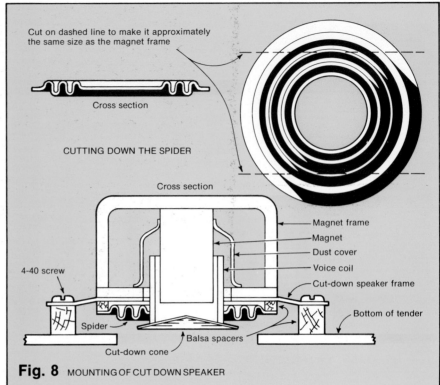

**Fig. 8** MOUNTING OF CUT DOWN SPEAKER

Another way of adapting a speaker to model dimensions was discussed by Peter A. Cook in the January 1971 MODEL RAILROADER. Figs. 7 and 8 show the method, which involves cutting down an ordinary 4" speaker to the dimensions of the magnet so you end up with a speaker about 1" wide and 1½" long.

The speaker is mounted to direct sound downwards. The magnet must be a demountable type so that you can clean off the iron filings after surgery (or remove the magnet beforehand). Avoid the kind of speaker that has a small cylindrical magnet assembly; they usually are swaged together and therefore difficult to reassemble correctly.

**Protection for the amplifier:** Pulse throttles can send part of their output into the output circuit of the cassette player, even through the capacitors that block d.c. Protection diodes must be added to the circuitry of the player-recorder to prevent damage to the transistors.

Fig. 9 shows the diodes, wired so that they do not normally conduct, added across the collector-to-emitter connection of the two output transistors. It may be a good idea to have a radio-TV serviceman do this work, since he probably has the service manual that tells which connection is which. Also add a 47-ohm resistor across the original speaker connections so that the cassette player can safely be left running even with no external speaker connected.

Early-model cassette players with internal output transformers cannot be protected this way. Add similar protection to a transistor phonograph ampli-

fier, if you use disks rather than tape.

Vacuum tube amplifiers do not need diode protection, but add the 47-ohm resistor across the speaker terminals.

**Throttle noise:** It is difficult to filter out the rectangular wave pulses generated in special purpose throttles such as the full performance throttle of Chapter 4. At low speeds the pulses create an annoying rattle in the speaker. More conventional throttles produce a hum, which is a little more tolerable because the frequency is in a range where the speaker isn't efficient. The rattle is the more persistent of the two problems, because the rectangular wave form contains many high-frequency components.

You can reduce the rattle or hum by

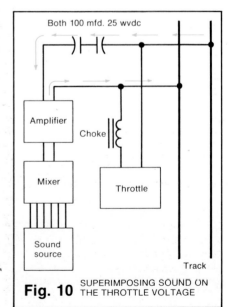

**Fig. 10** SUPERIMPOSING SOUND ON THE THROTTLE VOLTAGE

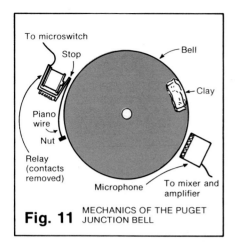

**Fig. 11** MECHANICS OF THE PUGET JUNCTION BELL

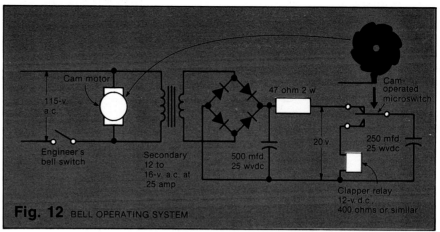

**Fig. 12** BELL OPERATING SYSTEM

reducing the value of the capacitors in series with the speaker. The limit is about 25 mfd. each. There will be a reduction in low-frequency sound, since the capacitors and speaker can't distinguish between good sound and bad noise.

### Synchronized sound

The Puget Junction display, first demonstrated at the 1965 NMRA convention by Herb Chaudiere, was one of the first layouts to demonstrate a synchronized exhaust sound and engineer-controlled whistle and bell. The system used hidden sound-effects equipment and electronic circuitry to produce the sounds. An electronic mixer blended the sounds — bell, whistle, steam hiss, and exhaust chuff — which then were amplified and conducted to the locomotive along with the throttle voltage (fig. 10). The speaker was in the tender. This brief description of the system is intended as a guide for experimentation. For a complete description, see the May 1966 issue of MODEL RAILROADER.

**Sound effects:** The bell and whistle noises were generated mechanically by equipment in soundproof boxes. Microphones picked up the sound for transmission to the mixer.

Finding an object with a suitable bell sound may be difficult. Chaudiere used part of a chandelier. Once you find a likely object, experiment with a bit of tape or modeling clay on the item to change the sound. For a clapper, Chaudiere used a piece of wire, with a small nut soldered to one end and attached at the other end to a relay (fig. 11). The relay was powered by a simple capacitor-discharge circuit controlled by a cam-operated microswitch. The timing of the bell was determined by the speed of the cam motor and the spacing of the lobes of the cam. (fig. 12).

The whistle used in the Puget Junction display was an air-operated three-chime whistle made from tubing, film cans, and a typewriter ribbon can (fig. 13). Air was supplied by a quiet squirrel-cage blower.

The Puget Junction sound system included a steam-hiss sound to mask gear

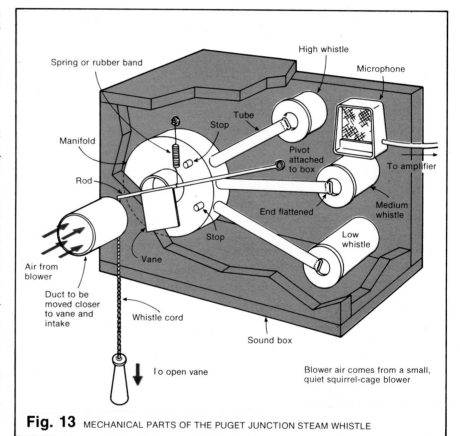

**Fig. 13** MECHANICAL PARTS OF THE PUGET JUNCTION STEAM WHISTLE

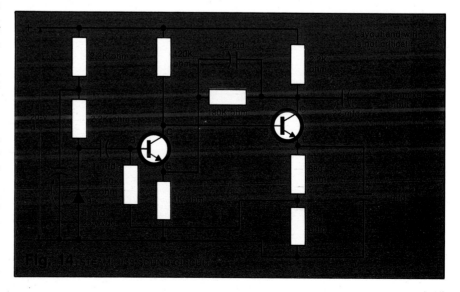

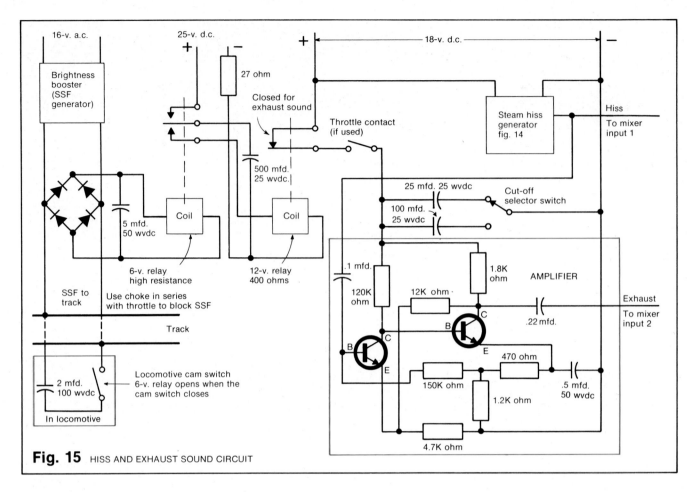

**Fig. 15** HISS AND EXHAUST SOUND CIRCUIT

noise and also to fill in with sound when the locomotive was stationary. This system used vacuum tubes; a transistor circuit with the same function is shown in fig. 14. Basically, the random noise in a zener diode is amplified by a pair of small transistors. Ordinarily the transistors would provide enough noise, but the zener diode prevents the direct pick-up of any local radio station. (If you still have a problem with AM or FM breakthrough and you can't convince yourself the engineer has a radio in the cab, enclose the entire noise generator in a grounded metal box.)

The exhaust sound was produced by a four-lobed cam on the driver axle which actuated a relay that interrupted the exhaust sound. The sound was generated in the same way as the steam hiss. The use of a second relay and a capacitor discharge unit in the circuit prevented a steady whoosh of exhaust sound if the engine stopped with the cam contacts closed (fig. 15).

**Electronics:** A complete discussion of the electronics of the Puget Junction sound system is beyond the scope of this book. Many of the mechanical parts must be made up, and much of the circuitry depends on the space available in the tender. Some modifications are suggested. The Brightness Booster of Chapter 8 can be used as the high-frequency oscillator in the switching of the "chuff," and a simple transistor mixer circuit (fig. 16) replaces the public-address type mixer. Fig. 17 shows the complete system. The wavetraps used in place of chokes, when using the 200-khz. high-frequency generator, actually are tuned resonant circuits. The Puget Junction display used .1-millihenry low-resistance coils paralleled by selected capacitors of about .003-mfd. rating. With the Brightness-Booster version fixed chokes replace the wavetraps in two positions and can be omitted for the headlight and the throttle.

Fig. 17 also shows a switch on the throttle control. With a momentum throttle control you could possibly have a contact arrangement operated from the control shaft so that cut-off capacitors automatically change as the throttle opens or closes.

## PFM sound system

Pacific Fast Mail of Edmonds, Wash., has made available an all-electronic sound system. It provides exhaust chuff, steam hiss, whistle, and bell sounds. The unit includes a transistor throttle and constant lighting for the locomotive. Furnished with the unit is paint for making the exhaust-synchronizing switch on the inside of one of the drivers. Recent PFM models have such a switch built in.

## Self-contained sound

By now you realize that all sound systems for model railroads are compromises. The best sound quality demands speakers that are too large to be contained in the locomotive, and if you send sound through the rails, it becomes impossible to use high-frequency constant lighting generators. The ideal sound system would be a self-contained unit, small enough to fit even an N scale locomotive.

Despite the miniaturization of electronic components, you must still count on using loudspeakers 1½" in diameter and 1" deep. Compatibility of these dimensions with 9-mm. track gauge is poor.

Because of this space problem, the system shown here is for O scale use. A 9-volt battery and a 1½" speaker are needed in addition to the electronic components. The system would be nearly impossible to fit into an HO tender, but you could use a hi-cube box car coupled to the locomotive (fig. 18).

Fig. 19 shows the sound installation in the tender of A.H.M.'s O scale Indiana Harbor Belt 0-8-0. No special attempt has been made at miniaturization, so the electronics practically fills the tender space. The 9-volt battery is carried under the coal load, and the off-on switch is right behind the coal bunker. Steam hiss is generated by a high-gain transistor and zener-diode amplifier, as in the previous section. The chuff or exhaust sound is generated by amplifying the irregular contact resistance noise caused by a rubbing electrical contact on a drive wheel or axle. Insulating tape provides the synchronized interruption.

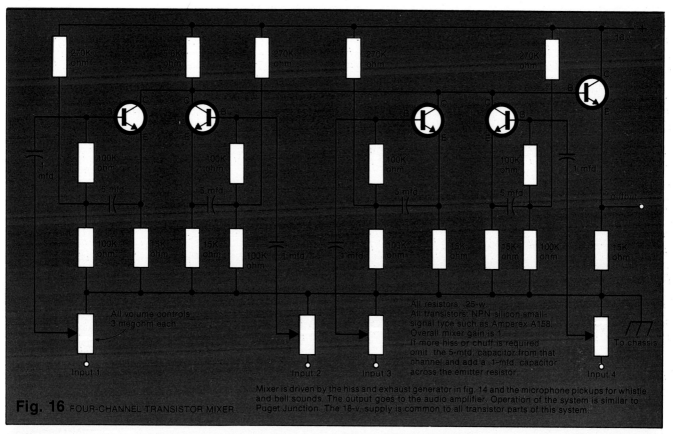

**Fig. 16** FOUR-CHANNEL TRANSISTOR MIXER.

Labels within figure: 270K ohm, 5.6K ohm, 270K ohm, 270K ohm, 270K ohm, 18-v. +, .1 mfd., 100K ohm, 100K ohm, 100K ohm, 100K ohm, 1 mfd., 5 mfd., 5 mfd., 5 mfd., 5 mfd., output, 100K ohm, 15K ohm, 15K ohm, 100K ohm, 1 mfd., 1 mfd., 100K ohm, 15K ohm, 15K ohm, 100K ohm, 15K ohm, All volume controls 3 megohm each, Input 1, Input 2, Input 3, Input 4, To chassis

All resistors ½-w.
All transistors: NPN silicon small-signal type such as Amperex A158.
Overall mixer gain is 1.
If more hiss or chuff is required omit the 5-mfd. capacitor from that channel and add a .1-mfd. capacitor across the emitter resistor.

Mixer is driven by the hiss and exhaust generator in fig. 14 and the microphone pickups for whistle and bell sounds. The output goes to the audio amplifier. Operation of the system is similar to Puget Junction. The 18-v. supply is common to all transistor parts of this system.

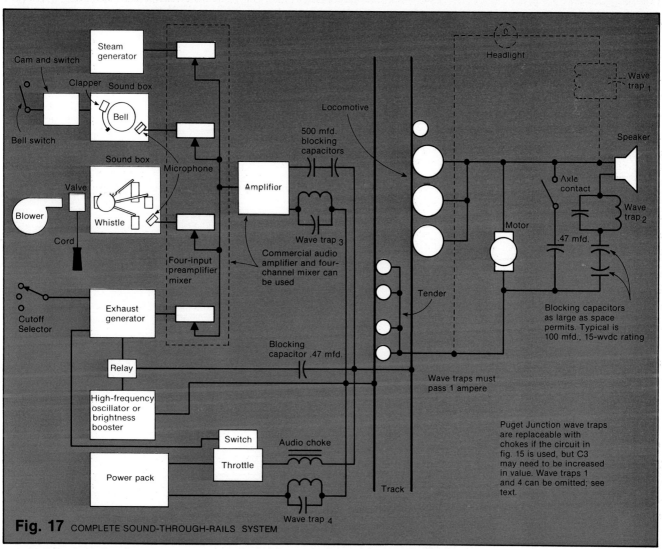

**Fig. 17** COMPLETE SOUND-THROUGH-RAILS SYSTEM

Labels within figure: Cam and switch, Clapper, Sound box, Steam generator, Bell switch, Bell, Valve, Sound box, Microphone, Blower, Whistle, Cord, Cutoff Selector, Exhaust generator, Four-input preamplifier mixer, Relay, High-frequency oscillator or brightness booster, Switch, Throttle, Audio choke, Power pack, Wave trap 4, Amplifier, 500 mfd. blocking capacitors, Wave trap 3, Commercial audio amplifier and four-channel mixer can be used, Blocking capacitor .47 mfd., Locomotive, Tender, Track, Headlight, Wave trap 1, Speaker, Axle contact, Motor, Wave trap 2, .47 mfd., Blocking capacitors as large as space permits. Typical is 100 mfd., 15-wvdc rating, Wave traps must pass 1 ampere, Puget Junction wave traps are replaceable with chokes if the circuit in fig. 15 is used, but C3 may need to be increased in value. Wave traps 1 and 4 can be omitted; see text.

Fig. 18. Battery, speaker, amplifier, mixer, and hiss generator are a snug fit in an HO scale hi-cube box car. Leads go to the locomotive.

Both the hiss and the chuff pass through a mixer to a small transistor amplifier, which in turn drives the speaker. Except for the exhaust-synchronizing contact, all the equipment is carried in the tender. Flexible wires and a small plug and socket connect the electronic components with the contact on the locomotive.

**The circuit** is shown in figs. 20 and 21. The complete power amplifier is not shown, since this normally will be a purchased item. Specify a 1-watt amplifier for 9-volt battery operation into an 8-ohm speaker. The input impedance of the amplifier should be 20,000 ohms or less, and the sensitivity for full output should be 20 mv. or less. Also, the amplifier should be a positive live, negative ground type to be compatible with mixer polarity. If you can get only a negative live, positive ground type, reverse the polarity of all the connections in fig. 21. Reverse the electrolytic capacitors in the mixer and the hiss amplifier, reverse the zener diode connections, and use PNP transistors instead of NPN.

The hiss amplifier and the mixer circuit can be handwired, as the layout is in no way critical. You can use a PC board, as in fig. 19.

**Exhaust contact:** A.H.M.'s mechanizing kit for the 0-8-0 switcher includes a spare phosphor-bronze electri-cal pick-up wiper. Mount it so it lightly contacts the axle of one of the two sprung drivers (fig. 22). The other contact for the switch is made by soldering a wire to the driver springing plate. This is the uninsulated wire showing in fig. 22. On some locomotives it may be more convenient to have the wiper rub along the periphery of a metal driver. In that case, one side of the exhaust contact

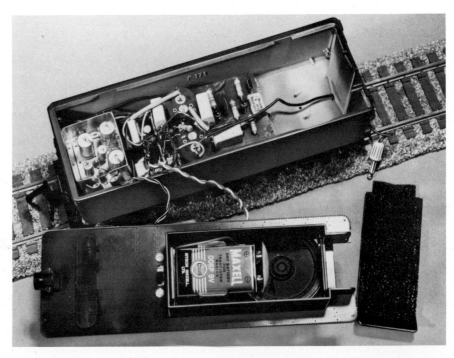

Fig. 19. Sound circuitry can be mounted in the tender of an O scale 0-8-0. For ease of replacement, the battery is positioned in the coal bunker.

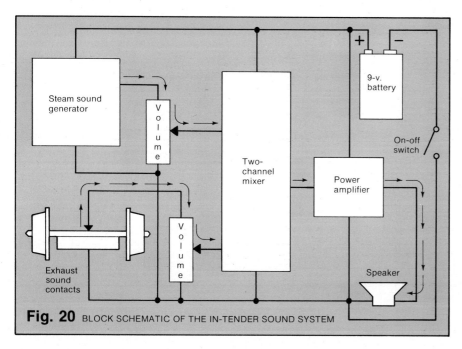

**Fig. 20** BLOCK SCHEMATIC OF THE IN-TENDER SOUND SYSTEM

switch is connected to the track pickup for that side.

To interrupt the exhaust noise, place pieces of thin vinyl insulating tape on the wheel or the axle — four for a conventional two-cylinder locomotive and six for a three-cylinder engine such as the IHB 0-8-0.

There must be no electrical contact between any part of the sound system, battery, or speaker and any metal part of the locomotive or the tender.

**Motor spark interference:** This type of circuit is particularly prone to pick up radiated motor noise and superimpose it on the exhaust sounds. Metal-bodied engines are less likely to encounter this difficulty than plastic ones. If the problem occurs, make sure that the motor brushes are in good condition and that the motor is properly run in. Add a capacitor across the motor brushes — a .047-mfd. ceramic disk type will do.

In extreme cases enclosure of either

the motor or the amplifier in a copper, brass, or tinplate shielding box may be necessary. If the amplifier is shielded, connect the shield to the common-battery-supply side that goes to one of the chuff switch contacts.

**Improvements to the system:** The self-contained sound system doesn't have a whistle or a bell. These could be piped in from trackside as in the Puget Junction system. You'd need to find room for another speaker.

John Armstrong described* a special switching system that senses drawbar pull so the exhaust sound can be muted for downhill or lightly loaded situations and raised to full volume for hard pulling. When the drawbar is compressed, the hiss of escaping steam comes in at full volume as though the locomotive were popping off.

Figs. 23 and 24 illustrate Armstrong's system. Modified relay contacts, normally closed when the locomotive is coasting, throw 1-ohm resistors across separate loudspeakers for steam and exhaust, cutting down volume considerably. The spring coupler of the tender, when compressed, opens the switch contacts controlling steam-hiss volume, and full-steam noise cuts in.

A slotted cam and follower are used to operate the contacts for exhaust sound. When the coupler is extended these contacts open for the full exhaust sound.

* MODEL RAILROADER, July and August 1969.

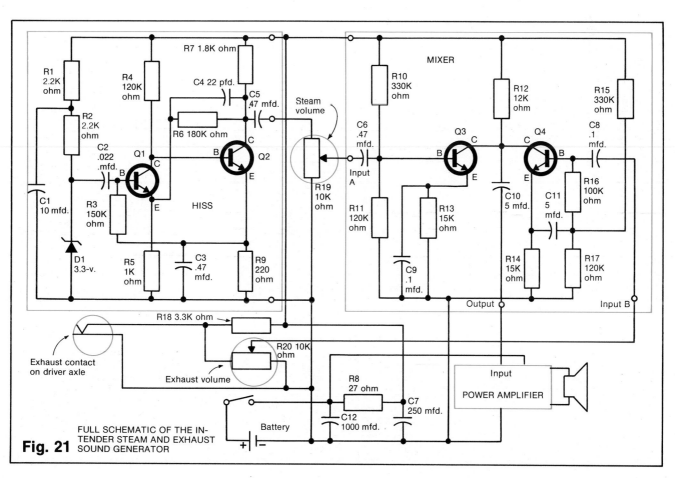

**Fig. 21** FULL SCHEMATIC OF THE IN-TENDER STEAM AND EXHAUST SOUND GENERATOR

## PARTS FOR STEAM AND EXHAUST SOUND GENERATOR

| | |
|---|---|
| Q1-Q4 | NPN silicon transistors rated at 25 volts and 100 mw., such as Sylvania ECG123A or Philips (Canada) BC108. |
| D1 | 3.3-volt, 250-mw. zener diode, such as 1N476A or Philips (Canada) BZY88/C3V3. |
| R1, R2 | 2200-ohm carbon resistors. |
| R3 | 150,000-ohm carbon resistor. |
| R4 | 120,000-ohm carbon resistor. |
| R5 | 1000-ohm carbon resistor. |
| R6 | 180,000-ohm carbon resistor. |
| R7 | 1800-ohm carbon resistor. |
| R8 | 27-ohm carbon resistor. |
| R9 | 220-ohm carbon resistor. |
| R10, R15 | 330,000-ohm resistors. |
| R11, R17 | 120,000-ohm resistors. |
| R12 | 12,000-ohm resistor. |
| R13, R14 | 15,000-ohm resistors. |
| R16 | 100,000-ohm resistor. |
| R18 | 3300-ohm resistor. |
| VR1 | 10,000-ohm potentiometer. |
| VR2 | 10,000-ohm potentiometer. |
| C1 | 10-mfd., 10-wvdc electrolytic capacitor. |
| C2 | .022-mfd., 100-wvdc ceramic or polyester capacitor. |
| C3 | .47-mfd., 100-wvdc polyester capacitor. |
| C4 | 22-pfd. ceramic capacitor. |
| C5, C6 | .47-mfd., 100-wvdc polyester capacitor. |
| C7 | 250-mfd., 10-wvdc electrolytic capacitor. |
| C8, C9 | .1-mfd., 100-wvdc polyester capacitors. |
| C10, C11 | 5-mfd., 50-wvdc electrolytic capacitors. |
| C12 | 1000-mfd., 10-wvdc electrolytic capacitor. |
| S1 | Dp.dt. miniature slide switch. |
| LS | Loudspeaker 1½″ in diameter, with impedance to suit the amplifier used. |
| Amplifier | 9-volt, 500-mw. miniature amplifier. |
| Battery | 9-volt battery with holder. |
| | All resistors can be .1-watt types with 5 per cent or 10 per cent tolerance. Polyester and ceramic capacitors can have 20 per cent tolerance rating; electrolytics, 50 per cent. |

Fig. 22. On the second axle can be seen the rubbing contact and the bit of vinyl insulating tape that interrupts the electrical continuity, creating the exhaust sound.

The cam has several slots to cope with varying train loads, and operates back on one side, forward on the other.

Armstrong's system is for O scale or larger. There just isn't room in HO, and the coupler does not have enough fore-and-aft range. Even in O scale, the three coupler springs require careful selection.

This mechanical linkage can be made to operate the single speaker system.

Fig. 25 shows the insertion points for the switch contacts. Electronically speaking, the circuit of fig. 25 is safer than the switching system of fig. 24, since the connecting of low-value resistors across loudspeakers in small transistor amplifiers results in increased battery drain and possible transistor overheating.

### Opto-electronic sound control

Another method of controlling exhaust loudness is illustrated in fig. 26. It is not as good as a drawbar-pull sensing system, but it does make the exhaust loudness proportional to the throttle voltage and therefore the speed. The volume change is incorporated by using a coupled light and cadmium sulfide photocell, so that the brighter the light, the lower the resistance of the photocell and the higher the volume of the sound.

The light is supplied with current from the motor terminals. The supply is filtered to eliminate transistor throttle pulses which might otherwise be picked up on the sound system by modulation of the photocell.

The Optel OSS302 opto-electronic control package works well for this purpose. It is enclosed in a light-proof case about .75″ x .75″ x .625″. The light draws 15 ma. at 10 volts. Cell resistance is 10 million ohms dark and 100 ohms lit. Some adjustments may be needed to the resistor bridging the photocell connections. A lower value here gives more sound at low throttle.

**Battery:** A 1-watt amplifier presents a heavy load to the battery. If battery life is a problem, current consumption can be reduced by using a 3.3- or 6.8-ohm, 1-watt resistor in series with the speaker connection. The volume of sound will be somewhat less. Alkaline batteries last longer than the conventional type.

In principle, the system also could be powered by the high-powered SSF generator described in Chapter 8, using a 9-volt zener diode and a rectifier with a filter capacitor. The exhaust contact would need to be completely isolated from the wheels and rails. Exhaust synchronization would require a cam and a microswitch or metal segments applied to an insulated wheel.

### Simultaneous control

One of the first difficulties the beginner encounters in model railroading is operating two trains on the same track. HOW TO WIRE YOUR MODEL RAILROAD by Linn Westcott has become a standard reference for the explanation of the cab control system. In effect, the cab control system involves splitting up the layout into electrically isolated sections of track. Switches permit a choice of the throttle or power pack connected to each section of track. Thus two trains can be controlled independently, assuming no operator error.

How much simpler, many have thought, if no gaps or block switches

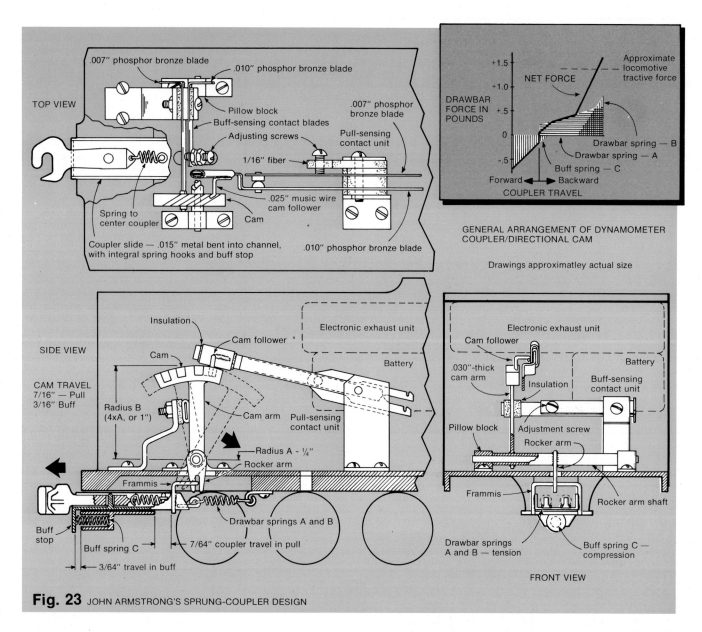

**Fig. 23** JOHN ARMSTRONG'S SPRUNG-COUPLER DESIGN

were necessary, and the rule of one speed and direction control for each locomotive existed, regardless of its location on the track.

In theory there are several ways to accomplish this electronically. Radio control is one way. Another might be to have the rails carry d.c., a.c., and SSF and have each locomotive tuned for one supply. However, the need for pulsed d.c. for starting and filtered d.c. for running plus polarity reversal would result in several kinds and directions of d.c. on the same rails. They would cancel each other out.

Therefore, a constant-voltage a.c. must be supplied to the track and a complete throttle control and reversing switch must be placed in each locomotive. Now radio control is possible, but the problems of space, antenna location, a servo motor for the throttle, and a relay for reversing are enormous — to say nothing of the cost.

About the only practical solution to have evolved commercially in terms of size, cost, and performance is General

Electric's Astrac system. In essence this involves a small SCR throttle in the locomotive. Astrac is not radio-controlled, but the SCR devices are turned on by high-frequency pulses superimposed on the constant 20- to 24-volt, 60-hertz a.c. track voltage. Each miniature receiver is tuned so that the pulses that turn it on do not interfere with the other receivers. Up to five locomotives can be operated simultaneously with Astrac, but in theory the system could be expanded.

Although other systems have been suggested, almost invariably one of two drawbacks is present. Either the motor is supplied with filtered d.c., which limits the niceties of slow running, or there are reversing complications that are either left unresolved or more complex in resolution than the situation deserves.

### Time-shared multiplex control

A noteworthy recent addition to the field of "simultraineous" control is the Digitrack 1600 command control system, manufactured by Electroplex, Inc.,

P.O. Box 82, Urbana, OH 43078. The Digitrack 1600 is a complex system that can control up to 16 locomotives at once. Technically it's a time-shared multiplex system, with the advantage over Astrac-type systems that the controlling pulses are derived from solid-state counters and the system is not in danger of going out of tune. It uses a constant 13 volts d.c. on the track, so like Astrac it provides the benefit of constant lighting.

The Digitrack 1600 system sends a precisely timed series of control pulses into the rails along with the filtered d.c. A group of 16 pulses goes out 100 times each second. The receivers in the locomotives have an integrated-circuit clock and counter, and the receiver responds to only one of the 16 pulses. The width and timing of the pulse control the speed and direction of the train. The term "time-sharing" means that control signals are sent out sequentially rather than simultaneously; "multiplex" means that several signals use the same circuit.

The Digitrack 1600 system comprises

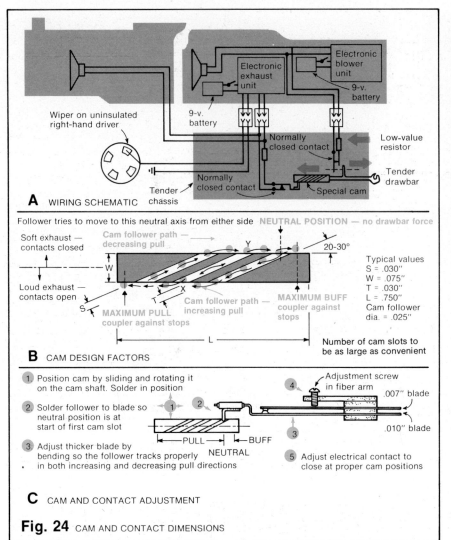

**A** WIRING SCHEMATIC

Wiper on uninsulated right-hand driver

Electronic exhaust unit

Electronic blower unit

9-v. battery

9-v. battery

Normally closed contact

Low-value resistor

Normally closed contact

Tender drawbar

Tender chassis

Special cam

Follower tries to move to this neutral axis from either side    NEUTRAL POSITION — no drawbar force

Soft exhaust — contacts closed

Cam follower path — decreasing pull

Loud exhaust — contacts open

Cam follower path — increasing pull

MAXIMUM PULL coupler against stops

MAXIMUM BUFF coupler against stops

20-30°

Typical values
S = .030"
W = .075"
T = .030"
L = .750"
Cam follower dia. = .025"

Number of cam slots to be as large as convenient

**B** CAM DESIGN FACTORS

1. Position cam by sliding and rotating it on the cam shaft. Solder in position
2. Solder follower to blade so neutral position is at start of first cam slot
3. Adjust thicker blade by bending so the follower tracks properly in both increasing and decreasing pull directions

PULL — BUFF — NEUTRAL

4. Adjustment screw in fiber arm
.007" blade
.010" blade

5. Adjust electrical contact to close at proper cam positions

**C** CAM AND CONTACT ADJUSTMENT

**Fig. 24** CAM AND CONTACT DIMENSIONS

a master power pack, which operates on 115-volt a.c. and supplies 4.5 amps at 13 volts (up to three auxiliary packs can be added, each supplying another 4.5 amps), control boxes with speed and direction controls, and receivers, which measure ¾" x 1" x 1¾". The basic system can control four locomotives; parts can be added to it to a maximum of 16.

Like Astrac, Digitrack 1600 is not compatible with sound-in-rails systems because the sound frequencies may interfere with the speed and direction pulses. Those pulses will be reproduced in the speaker. If you can find room, the battery-operated self-contained sound system can be used. It can be powered from the constant d.c. track voltage by dropping it to battery voltage with a zener diode and a resistor and by installing a protection diode to protect the sound system from reverse polarity, which might occur in reversing loops.

**Carrier control limitations:** The momentum and brake features of a good transistor throttle are incompatible with a carrier-control system like Astrac or Digitrack 1600. However, a constant track voltage is available for lighting. Too many lights may bleed off the high-frequency signal, since it will pass through the lamps. Then, too, be sure to compensate for the higher-than-normal track voltage by placing a resistor in series with each lamp — between 100 and 220 ohms, and about 1 watt.

Home construction of a carrier control system is not recommended. Special equipment is needed for tuning it.

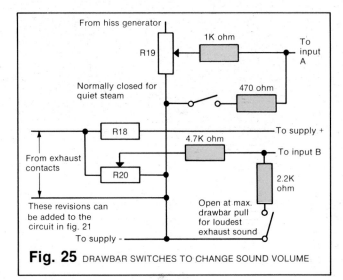

**Fig. 25** DRAWBAR SWITCHES TO CHANGE SOUND VOLUME

From hiss generator

R19

1K ohm

To input A

Normally closed for quiet steam

470 ohm

R18

To supply +

4.7K ohm

To input B

From exhaust contacts

R20

2.2K ohm

Open at max. drawbar pull for loudest exhaust sound

These revisions can be added to the circuit in fig. 21

To supply -

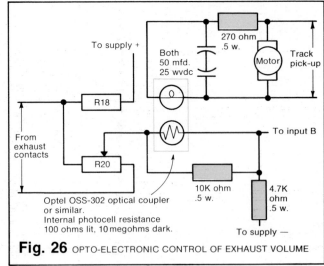

**Fig. 26** OPTO-ELECTRONIC CONTROL OF EXHAUST VOLUME

To supply +

270 ohm .5 w.

Both 50 mfd. 25 wvdc

Motor

Track pick-up

R18

To input B

From exhaust contacts

R20

10K ohm .5 w.

4.7K ohm .5 w.

Optel OSS-302 optical coupler or similar. Internal photocell resistance 100 ohms lit, 10 megohms dark.

To supply —

# ⑩ Commercial transistor throttles

EVERYONE can see or hear the results of your electronic circuitry, but the circuitry itself can remain hidden beneath the scenery or under the benchwork. Its actual appearance is unimportant. However, there is one device that is exposed to view: the throttle. If you are more inclined to buy than to build this foreground necessity, whether because you feel diffident about your abilities or simply because you lack time, you will find some helpful information in this chapter.

Transistor throttles, like automobiles, come in a variety of models and offer a wide range of optional equipment. As with the products of Detroit, the extras cost more. You may want to decide which features are the most important to you before you go shopping for a throttle.

Safety equipment is important. A circuit breaker protects both your locomotives and the throttle itself in the event of a short circuit. An off-on switch is a convenience which eliminates the necessity of unplugging the unit when you are not using it.

Classifiable as both safety and horsepower is the rating of the throttle. Be sure the throttle you choose can furnish the amount of current your locomotives and trains require. A 1-amp rating is sufficient for N scale and average HO scale duty. If your HO railroad, though, specializes in double-headed 50-car freights or long lighted passenger trains, a 2-amp rating is necessary.

All automobiles have brakes; not all transistor throttles do. Similarly, momentum is universal in automobiles (a result of physics rather than Detroit engineering) but not in transistor throttles. Both are good features in a transistor throttle, because they enhance the realism of operation. As you operate your railroad, you'll feel much more like a real engineer if, instead of simply turning the speed control down to zero, you have to manipulate a brake handle to bring the train to a stop. Pulsed power is also a desirable feature in any throttle, transistor or not. It functions as a low gear to facilitate smooth starting.

Most commercial throttles use circuitry similar to the three-transistor unit in Chapter 4. Some throttles operate on 115-volt a.c. and can be plugged into any wall socket; others lack a transformer and therefore require low-voltage a.c. from an ordinary power pack. Read the instructions before you connect the wiring.

Magazines such as MODEL RAILROADER are an excellent source of information on commercial throttles, both in the advertisements and in the product-testing columns. Your hobby shop can help you choose a throttle. You generally can trust the dealer's advice — no retailer who intends to keep you as a customer will sell you a throttle you'll later regret having bought.

An excellent way to become acquainted with transistor throttles is to

The Pacematic is a Canadian-made throttle compact enough to be hand-held. It requires low-voltage a.c. from a separate transformer or power pack. The unit shown is rated at 2 amps; a 4-amp version also is available.

Model Railroader: A. L. Schmidt.

The Fyffe Electronics Model Railroad Engine Power— 2 Amp throttle operates on house current. The output of the throttle is square-wave d.c. at low speeds that gradually increases to pure d.c. at high speeds. Braking is controlled by a two-position center-off toggle.

The Hammant & Morgan Electran, made in England, contains a transformer and operates on house current. The unique center-off speed control replaces the conventional reversing toggle.

Kalmbach Books: A. L. Schmidt.

The MRC Controlmaster VI is a heavy-duty unit with NPN transistors. It offers momentum but lacks a separate brake control. Two reversing switches provide for reverse loops and wyes. The case permits several different mounting positions.

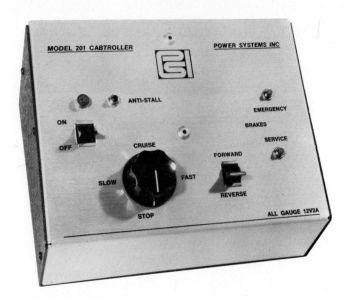

Codar throttles are available in several models. Some require low-voltage a.c., and others such as the TEC-80 are able to operate on house current. Most Codar throttles have a six-position switch that controls momentum and braking. The TEC-80 has been superseded by the TEC-88.

Power Systems markets the 200T uncased transistor throttle (below) and the 201 Cabtroller, which is the same unit in an aluminum case. The standard unit includes two brake buttons for service and emergency applications. An optional brake module shown with the 200T allows five prototypical braking rates.

find a friend who has one and try it out, possibly with one of your own locomotives. You know how that particular locomotive operates with your own throttle, and you can compare its behavior with the transistor throttle.

The transistor-throttle market is not static. Manufacturers upgrade and improve their products, and it is altogether possible, to use an imaginary example, that the Transithrott Mark II, which was the current model when this book was written, has been superseded by the Transithrott Mark IV-A. Then too manufacturers themselves enter and leave the field. Thus the commercial throttles pictured in this chapter may or may not be available at publication time. Nor should the fact that a throttle is pictured here be taken as a specific endorsement. Convenience — the particular throttle units that were on hand — more than any other factor guided the selection of throttles for this chapter.

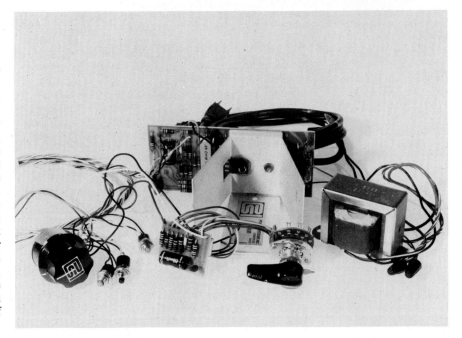

# Addenda

MOST of the answers and responses to readers' questions and comments about the first printing of this book are included in the body of this printing. A few items required more space than was available there; they are appended here.

If you find that the SCR throttle described on pages 23-26 provides acceleration that is too fast, increase R1 from 10K to 15K (15,000 ohms) or 22K to slow acceleration down somewhat. Similarly, if the brake action is too heavy, increase R2 from 3.3K to 4.7K or 6.8K. Alternately, both actions can be slowed by using a 1000-mfd. capacitor for C2 or connecting another 500-mfd. capacitor across the existing C2.

The dynaquad device specified on page 59 for the automatic horn control circuit may no longer be available. You can use a silicon-controlled switch, such as General Electric 3N58 or 3N83. Only three leads of the device—emitter (anode), anode gate, and collector (cathode)—are used. Two other modifications to the circuit are necessary. Replace R with a 100-ohm, .5-watt fixed resistor, and add a 270-ohm, .5-watt resistor in series with the collector (cathode) of Q1.

# Index

# Abbreviations

v.      volt
mv.     millivolt = .001 volt
a.      amp (ampere)
ma.     milliamp = .001 amp
w.      watt
mw.     milliwatt = .001 watt
hz.     hertz = cycles per second

khz.    kilohertz = 1000 hertz
d.c.    direct current
a.c.    alternating current
mfd.    microfarad
pfd.    picofarad = .000001 microfarad
wvdc    working volts d.c.
piv     peak inverse voltage

e.m.f.  electromotive force
K       1000
SCR     silicon controlled rectifier, thyristor
dp.dt.  double pole, double throw (switch)
3p.st.  three pole, single throw (switch)

# Symbols

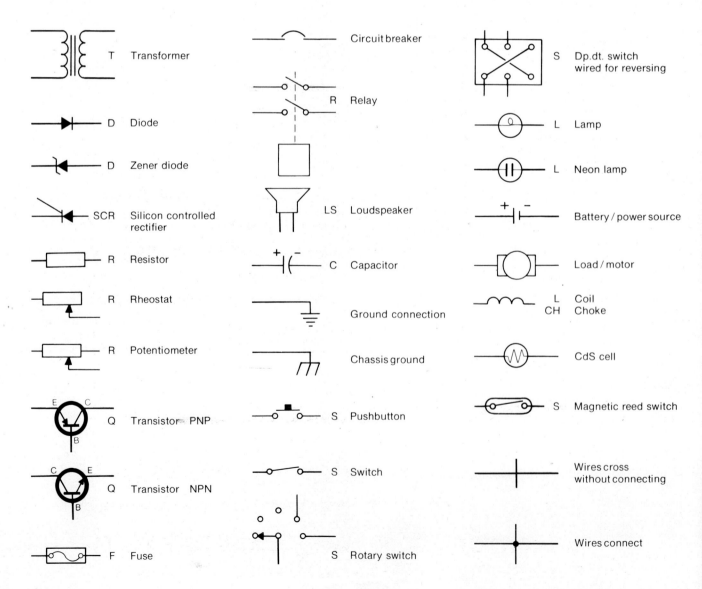

| | | |
|---|---|---|
| T — Transformer | Circuit breaker | S — Dp.dt. switch wired for reversing |
| D — Diode | R — Relay | L — Lamp |
| D — Zener diode | | L — Neon lamp |
| SCR — Silicon controlled rectifier | LS — Loudspeaker | Battery / power source |
| R — Resistor | C — Capacitor | Load / motor |
| R — Rheostat | Ground connection | L Coil / CH Choke |
| R — Potentiometer | Chassis ground | CdS cell |
| Q — Transistor PNP | S — Pushbutton | S — Magnetic reed switch |
| Q — Transistor NPN | S — Switch | Wires cross without connecting |
| F — Fuse | S — Rotary switch | Wires connect |